FIFTEEN INCH GAUGE RAILWAYS

Their History, Equipment, and Operation

DAVID MOSLEY
and
PETER VAN ZELLER

DAVID & CHARLES
Newton Abbot   London   North Pomfret (Vt)

The 'prehistoric' garden railway. *Lavinia* on Mr Fildes' line
in the woods of Lakeland in the 1860s. The tender shell
survives as an unlikely compost store! (*Dr R. Fildes*)

British Library Cataloguing in Publication Data

Mosley, David
Fifteen inch gauge railways: their
  history, equipment and operation.
  1. Railways, Miniature – Great
  Britain – History
  2. Railways, Narrow-gauge – Great
  Britain – History
  I. Title   II. Van Zeller, Peter
  385'.52'0941   TF675

  ISBN 0-7153-8694-8

Phototypeset by Typesetters (Birmingham) Ltd,
Smethwick, West Midlands
and printed in Great Britain
by Redwood Burn Ltd, Trowbridge
for David & Charles Publishers plc
Brunel House   Newton Abbot   Devon

Published in the United States of America
by David & Charles Inc
North Pomfret   Vermont 05053   USA

CONTENTS

CHAPTER ONE

SMALL BEGINNINGS

An Introduction

The Railway Age changed the face of Britain and extended the horizons of society. The railways created their own towns, standardised time, and provided all classes of people with an easy, quick means of travel. They made leisure and that splendid British institution, an excursion to the seaside, possible for the masses. Small wonder that trains have such an attraction for so many, and that model trains provided an introduction to something more than merely a form of transport for 'children of all ages'.

There have been model steam locomotives since the early days of railways, often built for sales promotion or instruction. The Norris Co built many large scale model locomotives which survive in museums in Paris and Vienna, but most influential was the 8ft long 4-4-0 of 1853, taken by Admiral Perry to the Shogun of Japan. In early 1854 the locomotive was steamed frequently, carrying children in a small coach and an official, named Egawa, on the roof. The latter later requested the Shogun's permission to be the first Japanese engine driver! The 22in gauge locomotive was destroyed by fire at Yokohama later in 1854. Nearer home a quarter scale model of a 2-4-0 'Crewe' type was built by Wilson's of Leeds in 1856 to represent to the Bombay, Baroda and Central India Railway the locomotives they would shortly receive. This 16½in gauge model still survives in the Science Museum vaults.

The first locomotive to a definite 15in gauge also survives, *Pearl*, built between 1859 and 1861 by Peter Brotherhood of the engineering firm of Chippenham, Wilts. The locomotive was a 2-2-2 of freelance outline, built robustly and certainly steamed. No records exist of a railway but a principal role was as a visual aid in an occasional lecture by Mr Brotherhood. *The North Wilts Herald* of 25 January 1862 commented:

A most interesting and instructive lecture . . . was delivered by Mr P. Brotherhood to a large and highly respectable audience . . . the lecture was remarkable not only for its explicit character, accompanied as it was by most beautiful diagrams and various illustrations together with a model engine made by the lecturer himself.

Pearl was donated to Kings College, London, (Brotherhood's old school) in 1915 and was restored to its former glory under the aegis of Sydney Leleux between 1959 and 1961.

Passenger carrying garden railways existed in various gauges at this period. The earliest recorded in a photograph was 300yd long running along a ledge on the wooded hillside above Far Sawrey in the Lake District. Charles Fildes, a Manchester manufacturer resident there, built the first private steam launch on Windermere in 1850 and the locomotive *Lavinia* soon afterwards. Local tradition had that the 2-2-2 locomotive used a steam launch boiler and engine unit and hauled firewood in two open wagons.

Another line of indeterminate gauge appears on the 1870 Ordnance Map of Argyll, running along the shores of Loch Fyne in the grounds of Ardkinglass House. The *Oban Times* of 9 October 1875 reported Queen Victoria's amusement:

A Model Railway – during Her Majesty's stay in the West, the Royal Party drove out and visited the property of Mr Callender to Ardkinglass . . . Mr Callender . . . is an enthusiast in mechanical contrivances which at first seem of little value but which on closer inspection are not only beautiful working models but really useful in various ways. For instance Mr Callender has, at considerable expense, erected a model railway nearly a mile in length, along the shores of Loch Fyne. Over this miniature line, a pygmy engine draws a handsome carriage capable of accommodating two persons. At intervals, stations have been erected and the line is worked on the most approved principles of a large railway system. The above carriage was designed and built by Mr Charles Thompson, coach builder, Glasgow. In addition Mr Callender has on his lake models of the Cunard steamer on which one might cross the lake.

The Tay Bridge Disaster night of 28 December 1879 saw extensive damage to the line and soon after George Callender was struck by mental illness, so that it was never restored. Today only the trackbed and the locomotive shed inspection pit remain between the loch shore and the artificial Caspian Lake. The locomotive was an 0-4-0 with a tall chimney, last seen in a garden in Tayvallich in 1912 where its boiler lay 40 years, later to be photographed for *Scottish Field*. Records place George Callender at Eton with one Arthur Percival Heywood, whose family took shooting on the estate at Glenfyne, and who was to develop the garden railway concept much further.

Small railways at this time also performed a transport need where it was impossible to install standard gauge tracks. Lead mines in Derbyshire had tracks with a gauge of less than 12in in their narrow adits, where loads of ore could be moved by manpower. Quarries and factories also had small gauge tracks, but the great revolution was the introduction of steam traction. In May 1862 an 18in gauge line was laid to carry internal traffic within the growing industrial complex of Crewe Locomotive Works. The tracks wove into existing buildings, round tight corners and were eventually extended to the station on a remarkable 220ft suspension bridge. *Tiny*, an 0-4-0T with 4¼ × 6in cylinders and 15¼in driving wheels, was designed by John Ramsbottom. It and four similar locomotives hauled 15 ton loads on four-wheeled cast framed trollies. Reorganisation in 1925 saw the loss of most of the system but *Pet* of 1869 survives in the Narrow Gauge Railway Museum at Tywyn.

The system was inspected later in 1862 by Charles Spooner, Engineer of the Festiniog Railway, before the introduction of steam locomotives on that line. Since 1836 this 13 mile track had hugged the hillside from Blaenau Ffestiniog to Portmadoc. The 23½in gauge and the use of horses to return empty wagons severely restricted the carrying capacity. Loco-

motive working began in 1863 closely followed by authorised passenger working, hitherto illegal on a gauge less than standard. The report to the Board of Trade commented

> The adoption of locomotive power on this little line is most important . . . the cheapness with which such a line can be constructed, the quantity of work that can be economically performed upon it and the safety with which the trains run on it, render it an example which will undoubtedly be followed sooner or later in this country, in India and in the Colonies, where it is desirable to form cheap lines for small traffic, or as a commencement in developing the resources of a new country.

The Festiniog was to be an example to the world but one man saw that:

> The marvel lies in the manner in which the work was adapted to the gauge, not in the suitability of the gauge to the work . . . so the question arises: what is the smallest and therefore the cheapest railway capable of being practically and advantageously worked?

Mr A. Percival Heywood was engaged on research into "a Comparative Estimate of Haulage by Steam on Light Railways and by Horses on Roads", for the Journal of the Royal Agricultural Society.

'Teacher's pet', on a plinth at King's College in the Strand, *Pearl* (1859–61), the earliest 15in gauge locomotive. (*Peter van Zeller*)

CHAPTER TWO

'THAT TIGHT LITTLE, LIGHT LITTLE RAILWAY'
The Work of Sir Arthur Heywood

If one man made the 15in gauge stand before other gauges, it was Arthur Percival Heywood of Duffield Bank in Derbyshire. His family were Manchester Bankers; his grandfather Benjamin was granted a Baronetcy for support of the 1832 Reform Act. Earlier Benjamin had been at Eccles Vicarage when William Huskisson was run down by the *Rocket*, and legend has his horse being used to take the black tidings to Liverpool. His son took their summer retreat at Dove Leys in Staffordshire as his home, where on Christmas Day 1849 Arthur Heywood was born. Arthur had an early interest in metalwork and while on vacation from Eton built a 4in gauge locomotive, then a 9in railway to carry his young brothers and sisters. He wrote later:

> The stability of this 9in line was perfect enough so long as persons did not attempt to ride on the ends and edges of carriages and wagons, but man being an article of approximately standard size, it is clear there must be a minimum gauge which will be stable enough to be independent of such liberties.

Experiments were to prove the 'Minimum Gauge' was to be 15 inches.

At Trinity College Cambridge Arthur achieved the first First Class Honours in the new discipline of Applied Science, probably because of his frequent illicit trips on the footplate where he learnt most of what there was to know about railway engines! After marriage he took a home at Duffield Bank, north of Derby, built a workshop and started to experiment with the minimum gauge concept. The justification was the need of the Royal Engineer Corps for a portable military railway system; the spur was the sight of John Barraclough Fell's eccentric system like a modern model engineer's elevated track, on which an 18in gauge locomotive ran, vulnerable to gunfire. Using mainly his own resources including a smithy, sawmill and foundry, he began in 1874 to lay a 15in gauge

line from the house to the main road to bring in materials. Then he built up into a cluster of gritstone quarries above the house with a 1 in 12 gradient and a 25ft radius curve.

The main line of the Duffield Bank Railway was over half a mile long shaped according to its builder 'like a pair of spectacles'. Northwards the first station at Manor Copse had covered accommodation for coaches. Then a 1 in 47 gradient, indicated by one of the set of lineside posts, took a sharp turn past the Rough station where a siding led to a rubbish tip – a splendid domestic application for the gauge. The line now approached its major civil engineering structure, a viaduct completed in 1878 from prefabricated parts, 91ft long and 20ft high. It was intended to show the Army what they were missing, and doubled as an anchorage for the children's garden swing! After Viaduct station came a 60ft tunnel leading to the main junction for another loop round a larger quarry via short overbridges, two more tunnels and Edgehill station. The line

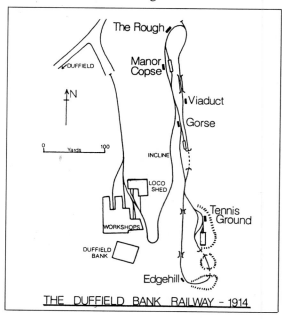

THE DUFFIELD BANK RAILWAY – 1914

Early days at Duffield Bank. *Effie* and earliest four wheeled stock approaching Edgehill. (*Sir Oliver Heywood*)

skirted a large tennis court where Tennis Ground Station formed the changing room. Here was a loop line and carriage shed.

The Duffield Bank Railway was laid using wooden sleepers, by Heywood, aided by two of the estate workers, at an average of 30yd a day. Later cast iron sleepers of Heywood's own design were standardised. He estimated that 2000yd of line plus an 0-4-0 locomotive and 12 wagons would cost £1800, with annual running costs of £250 and fuel costs of 5s (25p) a day. As the line was built, he used a diminutive 0-4-0 *Effie*, named after his wife as all Heywood locomotives were unashamedly feminine. Quickly built in six months, *Effie* drew heavily on the Crewe locomotives with its launch type boiler, though a simple rear wheel handbrake must have proved insufficient but exciting on the gradients. *Effie* ran at Duffield until 1894, was stored after and believed dismantled by the First World War. Rumours of it still persist – the Holy Grail of the Minimum Gauge!

Heywood's standard style of locomotive appeared with *Ella* of 1881, a handsome 0-6-0T with many unusual features including a flexible wheelbase. Victorian values were reflected in the open cab, Heywood arguing that a confined space was unhealthy, especially in an emergency, and 'a stout mackintosh is cheaper and far better for the driver'!

In the summer of 1881 the Royal Agricultural Society held its Annual Show at Derby and asked Heywood to open his line for inspection.

A pamphlet described the advantages of 15in gauge to tempt farmers, landowners and agents of the great estates with the vision of cheap transport; it remains a definitive source to this day. How many of the 128,000 visitors to the show went to Duffield is not known, what is sure is that no orders for such a railway came from the demonstration. This must have been a considerable disappointment for Heywood and the next decade was fallow for the Duffield Bank Railway. Instead Heywood explored other fields, the usual religious and philanthropic involvements of a responsible gentleman, and the art of bellringing for which he devised a roller bearing system for hanging church bells and founded the Central Council for Church Bell-ringers. The railway remained a family affair, operated by the children for Sunday School treats. It was a magnet for Victorian railway enthusiasts with the right social qualifications. There were public open days too with full timetables that cautioned 'none of the railway apparatus or rolling stock must be interfered with' and 'neglect of the following Regulations will be attended with risk'! The railway brought down timber, carried rubbish, and continued to be used for experiments by the military. By 1894, the line boasted a dining car and a sleeping car to 'test the capacity of the 15in gauge'. The 0-8-0T *Muriel* had just been completed to prove how powerful and fast a 15in gauge locomotive could be, weighing 5 tons to *Ella's* 3¾. In August another exhibition of the railway was held to promote the minimum gauge concept that traffic of 5-10,000 tons annually from estates, mines and institutions could be more economically carried by rail than road. It

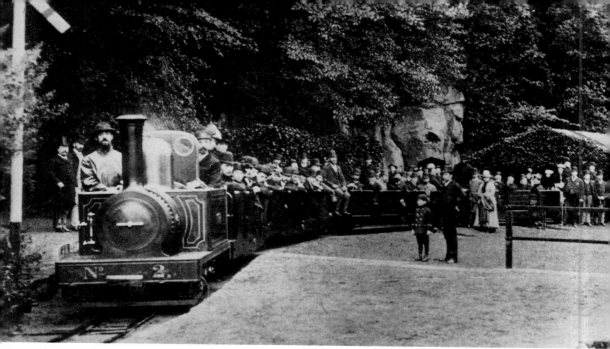

'A stout mackintosh . . .' The driver in obligatory apparel and *Ella* in original form at Tennis Ground on one of the open days at the Duffield Bank Railway. (*L&GRP/David & Charles*)

was viewed by the Hon Cecil Parker, agent to the 2nd Duke of Westminster, who saw its application to the needs of Eaton Hall, the Duke's estate near Chester. This vast stately home consumed 2000 tons of coal and over 3000 tons of general stores each year, brought by horse and cart from the Great Western Railway at Balderton. Outwards the estate sawmill, brickyard and pipeworks sent finished goods. The first and only manifestation of the Heywood Minimum Gauge Railway was about to take place.

The Duke agreed to the proposed line as long as it did not obtrude on his view, and Heywood surveyed the site during the arctic winter of 1894–5. He estimated £6,000 to construct the line, undertaking to oversee it personally to further his experience. In the end the cost was £5893-2s-11d; would that today's contractors could estimate so accurately! Track laying began in August 1895 from Balderton, and the social structure of Victorian England loomed large: 'on account of the large amount of game in the neighbourhood of the line, it was considered wiser to employ no contractor, nor were any men obtainable with a knowledge of such diminutive plate laying'.

Heywood commented later that 'For the first fortnight I worked away myself with beater, rammer and crowbar, till I had taught a proportion of my staff of 16 the use of these tools and how to put the permanent way together'. The highest standards were adhered to with sleepers in cast iron coated in anti-corrosion material, road crossings set in concrete, and all embankments turfed; intended to last 25 years, the line lasted 50.

The main line climbed steadily from Balderton to the Hall, crossing the main Wrexham road half way. Here trains were obliged to stop before crossing by the terms of the agreement with the local council. A branch led from here to the engine shed at Belgrave, and the estate works at Cuckoo's Nest. The main line followed the main drive unobtrusively through trees, and approached the Hall via a sharp curve by the cricket ground. At the terminus was a carriage shed, a large coal store and a branch to the generating station producing electricity for the Hall. Now much overgrown, the site is still recognisable today, the Eaton stock again residing in the Carriage shed.

The line was completed in September 1896 and was to be worked 'one engine in steam'. A four-wheeled tank engine *Katie* similar to the Duffield locomotives but without the flexible wheelbase, was finished like them in Holly green; 30 wagons with removable tops for either coal, brick or timber traffic, permanent way wagons, an open coach, a parcels van and a brake were provided and finished in milk chocolate livery. In full

The organisation at Duffield Bank is plain to see in this timetable and instruction notice for one of the open days. (*John Snell*)

operation, the line handled 6000 tons of material annually plus several hundred tons of peat to redesign the gardens. In 1897 running costs came to £239-12s-4d, with wages for the driver and boy of £115-12s-0d, an increase of 8s 4d on the previous year! Driver Wilde came from Duffield Bank and managed routine maintenance at the Belgrave shed, calling on Heywood or his fitter William Midgeley in an emergency. One such came in 1899 when *Katie*, always prone to slipping, broke down. *Muriel* was sent from Duffield for two years and two years later a new 0-6-0 arrived to be named *Shelagh*, the nickname of the new Duchess. This was an enlarged *Ella* and proved so suitable that another, *Ursula*, was ordered, though not completed until 1916.

From 1899 the new Duke encouraged use of the line, not just for freight but for guests to the Hall and shooting parties. Driver Wilde kept a notebook in which went the names of his exalted clientele, including King Edward VII, Queen Alexandra, King Alphonso of Spain and Mr Winston Churchill. The train took sportsmen to

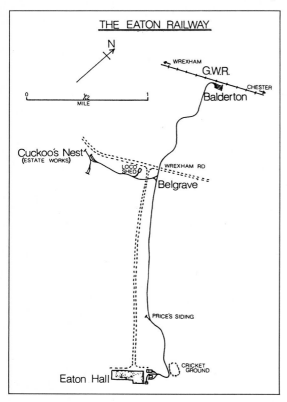

THE EATON RAILWAY

Katie on a passenger train at the Eaton Hall terminus in 1897 with Driver Wilde in control. The coal store (left) and the carriage shed still stand today. (*F Wilde*)

their butts and returned the unfortunate pheasants to the Keeper's lodge. Churchill commented 'I'd much rather play at trains.'

In 1905 the Eaton Railway became a proving ground for the future of the Minimum Gauge when the scale model 4-4-2 *Little Giant* was tested on its way from Bassett-Lowke's at Northampton to Blackpool Pleasure Beach. Its designer, Henry Greenly, was not so proud as to ignore the Heywood locomotives, though his employers always fettered him within the model image. Another of his designs was tested on the extended run at Eaton in 1914, the Bassett-Lowke Pacific *John Anthony*, owned by John Howey of Staughton Manor.

Meanwhile Heywood had inherited the family title in 1897 and the home at Dove Leys. Though another railway would have been a beguiling project, little work was done as Miss Effie Heywood, one of Sir Arthur's daughters, explained in a letter in 1974: 'There never was a railway at Dove Leys . . . there was a tramway (the same gauge as Duffield) that ran round the yards and small trucks were hand pushed'. Duffield Bank continued in operation until Sir Arthur's untimely death in April 1916. He had just sold some stock including the dining car to the newly re-opened Eskdale Railway and completed *Ursula* for the Eaton line, now carrying extra traffic to the military hospital established at the hall. Six weeks after his death, the railway at Duffield was auctioned in its entirety, including workshop equipment. Hill Bros of Derby, Metal Merchants, bought rails, stock

Both the officer and the young lady seem delighted with the arrival of *Ursula* at Eaton in 1916. The photograph is taken in front of the Belgrave locomotive shed which still stands as part of a garden centre. (*F Wilde*)

and many spares for £575 but whatever plans they had for running a pleasure line in wartime were dashed when *Ella* and *Muriel* were requisitioned. They went briefly to the huge munitions complex at Gretna where they hauled cordite before purpose-built fireless locomotives were obtained, so dire was the need for shells at that stage of the war!

The arrival of *Ursula* at Eaton came after the departure of *Katie* to the Eskdale line, having bequeathed her name to *Shelagh* following divorce in the Grosvenor family. After the war both locomotives were eclipsed by the arrival of a Simplex petrol locomotive in 1922.

Both steam locomotives suffered from tube trouble and Driver Wilde had lost the back-up of the Duffield Bank workshops, though *Ursula* continued in occasional use on high days and holidays. The estate staff watched the railway's progress with eagle eyes, faults were im-

mediately noticed and friendly rivalry between the railwaymen and the others was intense. The Simplex was replaced in 1938 by an updated model and both steam locomotives remained in store until they succumbed to a scrap drive in September 1942. The Cuckoo's Nest branch was lifted by the end of the war and the rest was sold with the stock to the Romney, Hythe & Dymchurch Railway in 1947.

So ended the Heywood era. Considered dispassionately it can only be considered a failure. Other countries adopted military and agricultural light railways with fervour. But Heywood had the misfortune to be operating in a period of agricultural depression while the opening of the Eaton Railway in 1896 co-incided with the repeal of the Red Flag Act which removed many restrictions on road transport. The Light Railway Act of that year did nothing to encourage the spread of cheap rail links by giving security of tenure for road crossings. However, the principle that 15in gauge was safe for passenger carrying so influenced the pleasure line promoters that the gauge became a recognised standard.

CHAPTER THREE

A CHANGE IN DIRECTION
The Influence of the Cagney Brothers

Across the Atlantic, the 15in gauge developed in an entirely different way from that promoted by Heywood. In the United States short passenger lines operated purely for pleasure in amusement parks and exhibitions. The main promoters were the Irish American brothers Cagney–Timothy, David, Charles and Thomas, who traded as the Miniature Railroad Company – 301 Broadway, New York City. They ambitiously offered 'any type of steam locomotive from 12⅝in to standard gauge' but standardised in 12⅝, 15, 18 and 22in gauges. A single prototype was used, the New York Central & Hudson Railroad 4-4-0 No 999 that had achieved unprecedented speeds with the Empire State Express in 1893, capturing the imagination of the American public. Though model sized, Cagney locomotives were built to work hard; initially they were built by

The Glasgow International Exhibition 1901. Patrons admire the first 15in gauge Cagney engine in the country. (Courtesy National Railway Museum)

the Cagneys' uncle, Peter McGarrigle of Niagara Falls, but later by the Hershell Spillman Co of nearby North Tonnawanda. Over 3,000 were built, including one entirely nickel plated for the King of Siam. However in 1926 American legislation required a licensed driver and fireman on all steam locomotives running in public. Steam vanished suddenly from funfairs and only a handful of the 4-4-0s survived in private hands or museums. The Miniature Railroad Co produced a petrol engined Pacific, but the demand for this was not enough to keep it in business.

In 1901, *The Railway Magazine* had reported:

> At Callao in Peru, a Class D 15in gauge train was established some time ago for regular passenger traffic between a local park and the city. The line was capitalised for £5,800 and pays a dividend of 25%.

Profit from pleasure caused similar developments in Britain, where a 12⅝in gauge train was

The 'iron horse' hauls a 'surrey with a fringe on the top'. This line at Alexandra Palace lasted from March 1903 until April 1904. (*Jeff Price*)

operated at the 1901 Earls Court Exhibition by a Captain Boyton. That year he operated a second Cagney 4-4-0 at the International Exhibition at Kelvingrove in Glasgow. It ran on 160yd of 15in gauge track with twice the capacity of the smaller line, proving 'the best patronised of all the model exhibits . . . the miniature railway train'. By May 1903 Boyton had negotiated a lease for some 200yd of 15in gauge track along the hillside at Alexandra Palace overlooking the main line out of Kings Cross. A 2d bell punch ticket was issued to ride in the Cagney's three coach train. Inside the Palace another International Exhibition displayed 'the spear that killed General Gordon . . . and the bugle that sounded the charge of the Light Brigade'. However the Palace Trustees were asking for the removal of the tracks by the following spring. Such equipment was so robust that it required little in the way of a special roadbed, and so light that it was easily moved. Other exhibitions followed, but records other than postcards are virtually non existent. These showed the same locomotive in 1907 on a track around the lake at the White City, Trafford Park, Manchester.

At this period another locomotive, distinguishable by its wagontop boiler as a Hershell Spillman, was used on a temporary line round the fountain in the Grand Central Walk at London's Crystal Palace. 'The Empire Express – the Smallest Train in the World' was run by W. H. Bond of Merrington Road, West Brompton, who had another line at Luna Park in Southend. The balloon loop track at the Kursaal Southend was operated by a Hershell Spillman engine in the 1920s until it was taken over by Nigel Parkinson in 1930. One of these locomotives ran at the 1913 Liverpool Exhibition, although at its opening in May the 500yd track was 'still in course of erection' alongside the Mountain Scenic Railway. So a small number of American engines virtually cornered the market for miniature railways at exhibitions in Britain, before the First World War.

In sharp contrast to these lines flung down for a fast buck, was one laid as suggested by *Railway Magazine* in 1901: 'on country estates, a miniature railway may have many uses besides that of amusement'. In 1903 a wealthy civil engineer, Charles Bartholomew, began the Blakesley Miniature Railway to connect Blakesley Hall, Northants, with the nearby station on the East and West Junction Railway. From Blakesley station yard a 15in gauge track followed the standard gauge under a road bridge, then climbed steadily at 1 in 100 crossing fields and streams to end at a corrugated iron depot behind the Hall. In the grounds a large circle of track made a triangular junction with the main line that was protected by electric banner signals. Stock comprised four bogie carriages converted at Blakesley from early

'An hilarious occasion' at Blakesley. *Blacolvesley*, the Cagney and a train of converted American coaches entertain the Railway Club in summer 1914. (*Philip Kingston*)

Cagney four-wheelers, and a standard 4-4-0 built in 1902. All contemporary accounts including Henry Greenly's record a single steam locomotive, although in 1906, *Model Engineer* had photographs of a second similar locomotive with stock like that used at Alexandra Palace. The Minimum Gauge traditions of visiting engines and confused researchers were thus upheld!

In 1905 Bartholomew scored a first for the Minimum Gauge. The steam locomotive was great fun for passenger work; however something instant was needed for goods traffic, particularly to bring coal up to the newly installed electric lighting plant at the hall. The estate engineer built *Petrolea* to Bartholomew's design using a small petrol engine on a 4-4-4 chassis. It proved powerful, fast but utilitarian in appearance. In 1909 the steam locomotive was loaned to Bartholomew's friend, Wenman J Bassett-Lowke, to run on a line at Crystal Palace, Sutton Coldfield. In part recompense, Bassett-Lowke's engineering works produced the elegant steam outline petrol-engined 4-4-4

Blacolvesley to designs by Henry Greenly. Ugly sister *Petrolea* was transformed in the following year to a steam outline by Bassett-Lowke. Both locomotives were used on estate work, the line having been extended to the family farm. Visitors would use the private telephone from the station to summon a train to collect them. Bartholomew was a great supporter of village events so that the annual flower show and fetes saw free rides for all, although proper Edmondson tickets were issued. 'An hilarious occasion' was the visit of the Railway Club in May 1914, whose train was hauled by the steam locomotive and banked by *Blacolvesley*.

After Bartholomew's death in 1919, his widow kept the line operational with the petrol locomotives. It was dismantled in 1939, and the surviving equipment was auctioned in Yorkshire in 1943. *Blacolvesley* and the distinctive coaches with their rail-built chassis actually met the Southend Hershell Spillman on the Redlands Railroad at Ponteland and the Newcastle Town Moor during the second world war. Only one other Miniature Railroad Co locomotive survived to run at Ettrick Bay in 1936, alas missing the vital building date from the smokebox front casting, and making its early history speculation.

CHAPTER FOUR
'A LINE FOR ALL REASONS'
The Work of Bassett-Lowke and Greenly

The Edwardian era saw the establishment of some lengthy and substantial pleasure lines, two of which survive 75 years later. The men who brought this about were Wenman J. Bassett-Lowke and Henry Greenly. 'Wynne' Bassett-Lowke was one of the renowned Northampton family of engineers and his model retailing business at the turn of the century popularised the model railway hobby in this country by supplying scale models that actually represented the real thing. He supplied parts and complete locomotives designed by Greenly, who had studied engineering and architecture at the Regent Street Polytechnic before joining the Metropolitan Railway in 1897 in the drawing office. He left to join the new Percival Marshall magazine *Model Engineer*, soon becoming its technical editor and then author of *The Model Locomotive*. In 1901 both men saw the American

15in gauge locomotive at the Glasgow Exhibition, and it must have irritated them, when Bartholomew ordered another for Blakesley Hall, as an opportunity wasted.

In 1904 'The Miniature Railways of Great Britain Ltd' was formed at Northampton for the purpose of manufacturing miniature locomotives and railways, and working them at exhibitions, public parks and pleasure grounds. The company also wished to provide material for 'equipping gentlemen's estates and parks with complete railways'. Bassett-Lowke was to be Managing Director with Greenly as engineer, and their first objective was to build a quarter-scale locomotive to match 15in track gauge accurately. A new large scale model shop was added to the Lowke premises and work began on the Class 10 4-4-2 *Little Giant* following the Atlantic type in use on the crack expresses of the day. Greenly's freelance design compared in beauty of form with the full size North Eastern Railway and Great Central Railway locomotives. Completed in 3½ months, *Little Giant* had the opportunity to show its paces en route to its intended site of operation at Blackpool. The

The first miniature locomotive trials at Eaton Hall in 1905. *Little Giant* stands at Balderton with the 12ton test train. The experimental nature of the occasion is emphasised by the gentleman with the note-book while Driver Smithies is at the regulator. (*John Snell*)

locomotive was unloaded at Balderton for a day's trial running on the Eaton Railway, in the presence of a band of highly regarded model engineers.

Operations began at Blackpool on Whit Monday 1905 and *Little Giant* proved an instant hit. In a week the maroon locomotive had travelled over 100 miles and pulled 9000 passengers on a ¼ mile circuit! At Gipsyville station the ticket office (adult fare 3d) had two staff with uniforms that would have graced the Royal Yacht. However, there was little interest among the 'thousands of admiring locomotive enthusiasts' for buying the British product at £345. Miniature Railways of Great Britain then developed a second line at Sutton Park, Sutton Coldfield. The 1907 season had been run by some earlier 10¼in gauge stock built by Smithies including an 0-4-4 tank engine named *Nipper*. By Easter 1908, the track had been regauged and run-round facilities provided for the second Class 10 *Mighty Atom*. This line operated successfully up to 1914 except for a tragic fatality when a boy was caught between the train and a bridge abutment.

'Entente Cordiale' was the theme of the next venue at the 1909 Exposition Internationale de l'Est de France at Nancy. Miniature Railways provided a mile of track which circled the site providing transport. Another Class 10 *Entente Cordiale* was finished in London, Brighton & South Coast Railway 'yellow' livery, but such was the success of the line that a second locomotive was soon needed. It was *Mighty Atom*, now repainted apple green and renamed *Ville de Nancy*, to the rescue. It was replaced briefly at Sutton Park by the Blakesley Cagney. Devotees of small trains were kept in the picture from 1909 when Greenly and Bassett-Lowke began to publish *Model Railways and Locomotives* a monthly magazine devoted to 'model railway construction and working'. Through to 1918 it acted as house journal for their activities.

Just before Easter 1909 an American syndicate ordered two Class 10 locomotives, one to be delivered in 36 working days. By July *Red Dragon* was operating the 'London–Paris Express' for the Side Shows Railway Ltd at the White City Imperial International Exhibition London. Another locomotive, *Green Dragon*, was not required to run but was on display.

In 1910 the Blackpool concession was not renewed because of the difficulties of running in the sandy conditions and the equipment was transferred to the grounds of Halifax Zoo at Chevinedge. This line needed a tunnel, embankment and 14ft high viaduct. *Little Giant* was fitted with a bogie tender, repainted green and renamed *Little Elephant*.

The 'London to Paris Express' on a wet day at the White City in 1909. The locomotive is Miniature Railways of Great Britain Ltd Class 10 *Red Dragon* and although the coaches seem ornate the uniform on the left is very much in Miniature Railways tradition. (*John Harrison*)

These doings paled into insignificance compared with the line at the International and Universal Exhibition at Brussels, which modestly described itself as 'THE Event of 1910'. There was a double track 'laid and finished in a way which would do credit to any crack English company' with a tunnel to 'impress passengers with that sense of damp, smoky gloominess, reminiscent of the old District or the Simplon subway'. The whole enterprise was under the control of Mr Trenery, Miniature Railways continental representative. Two trains were to shuttle to and fro and three locomotives were provided, patriotically named *King Edward, King Albert* and *King Leopold*. It is likely that only one was a new locomotive, the others being earlier locomotives renamed. There followed a line of continental ventures at Roubaix, Cologne and Breslau before the first world war, after which one Class 10 was discovered wrecked in a quarry behind the German front.

In April 1911, *Models, Railways and Locomotives* as it had become, announced 'plans have been passed by the Rhyl Town Council for a 15in gauge miniature railway round the lake in the Marine Park'. So came into being a line that was to be Miniature Railways' swansong and Greenly commented 'it is not often that the site

Henry Greenly stands by Driver Smithies who is driving *Prince Edward of Wales* on the Rhyl Miniature Railway in 1911. The fine station building is much in evidence and the Japanese naval ensign above the clock is witness to prevailing alliances. (*John Snell*)

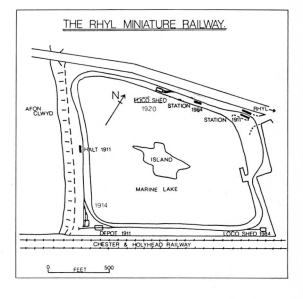

for a public miniature railway can be pronounced as ideal but the one at the Marine Park and Lake Rhyl, certainly comes within this category'. A circular track about a mile in length round the lake was provided with an elegant station on the north side. On the south side the track paralleled the LNWR Holyhead line and the steepest gradient was a mere 1 in 220. Six chocolate and cream coaches were provided and the locomotive *Red Dragon* was repainted Caledonian Blue and renamed *Prince Edward of Wales*. Contemporary postcards show Fred Smithies as Leading Driver and a prerequisite of Miniature Railways operations, Kelly, the railway dog.

The line opened on 1 May 1911 and one of the invited guests soon found himself driving the engine. J. E. P. Howey had just bought a 9½in gauge GNR Atlantic from Bassett-Lowke and now he had 'caught the 15in gauge bug'. Bank Holiday 7 August 1911 proved to be a record day following the arrival of two extra coaches. Trains ran from 9.05am to 10.15pm with scarcely a break. In the end 93 journeys carried 5003 passengers at fares of 3d for adults and 2d for children. The following year the line was taken

over by Rhyl Amusements Ltd which began a process of improvement. In 1913 the line's capacity was increased by using *George the Fifth* brought from Southport, and an additional train of 'bogie cars de luxe' built at Rhyl. The station was expanded with a loop, while a virtue was made of necessity by building a tunnel under the adjacent rollercoaster.

Miniature Railways of Great Britain Ltd went into voluntary liquidation in 1912, its assets being the lines at Halifax, Sutton Coldfield and the continental stock. Mr Trenery held onto the company name but did not trade as such.

W. J. Bassett-Lowke now had a new partner in Robert Proctor-Mitchell, heir to the Polytechnic Tours travel business. Together they formed Narrow Gauge Railways Ltd, with John Wills as company secretary. He was a solicitor who had retired early to indulge the delights of small trains. Together they were to change the course of the minimum gauge and follow the example of a recent American 18in gauge line at Venice, Los Angeles, to perform a public transport function. They commissioned Greenly to design new locomotives for Narrow Gauge Railways – initially advertised as Class 20 and 30 – sic – a much enlarged Atlantic and Pacific. However, before considering them, three other lines built to contract and equipped by Bassett-Lowke must be considered.

On 25 May 1911, a postman, Mr Griffin Llewelyn, opened the Llewelyn's Miniature

Class 30 Atlantic, *Synolda*, outside the depot of the Sand Hutton Railway in 1913. The Bassett-Lowke four wheeler and the home-produced 'Glass Coach' provide an interesting contrast in passenger vehicles. (*K. Hartley*)

Railway on the shore of the marine lake at Southport. It ran ½ mile from Lakeside 'adjacent to the Flying Machine' via a 'very realistic tunnel' to Pierhead. At first a Class 10 *George the Fifth* was employed but this was replaced in 1913 by the larger boilered improved Class 20 *Prince of Wales*. Rolling stock comprised open and closed bogie coaches and the 'Royal Saloon' reserved for special occasions and first class passengers, though it is doubtful if this tramlike vehicle ever carried royalty! It was intended to extend the line to 1¼ miles although this had to wait 35 years to come to fruition.

The Sand Hutton Railway near York was an estate line of an unusual type. It was constructed by Sir Robert Walker 'the richest man in the British Army' but despite the fact that he knew Sir Arthur Heywood, the line had no function but pleasure. It joined the Hall with the cricket pitch via a tunnel and a viaduct. To run the line, came the first example of Greenly's Class 30 Atlantic, named *Synolda* after Lady Walker, and some Bassett-Lowke four-wheel coaches, while a brake van and a saloon observation coach were built on the estate. The line was popular with visitors, used to the full for garden parties and fetes, and on some Sundays a train ride was the reward offered to tempt children to Sunday School.

The final step in Bassett-Lowke locomotive development took place in January 1914 with the completion of what was now called the Class 60 Pacific. 'The number of Pacifics has doubled overnight' enthused *The Railway Magazine* alluding to GWR 4-6-2 No 111 *The Great Bear*. The three-ton locomotive was built for Mr

'The number of Pacifics has doubled overnight'. Mr Howey's magnificent Class 60, soon to be named *John Anthony* at Staughton Manor in the spring of 1914. (*Courtesy National Railway Museum*)

J. E. P. Howey's Staughton Manor Railway in Huntingdonshire, which had been regauged from 9½in and its magnificent Greenly designed 'Forth Bridge' strengthened. With this most powerful 15in gauge locomotive, now named *John Anthony*, after his son, Howey looked to be able to run it on full regulator. A second bout of trials on the Eaton Railway came about and Cecil J. Allen later recalled the thrill of *John Anthony* flying along at 35mph in July 1914. Events overtook Howey and his Pacific while still at Eaton, and the locomotive remained in store for two years at Balderton. In 1916 it was purchased by Narrow Gauge Railways and renamed *Colossus* for service on the Eskdale Railway.

Narrow Gauge Railways Ltd had meanwhile been involved in two continental exhibition lines. In April 1912 Greenly was asked to design a line for the Luna Park in the Parc des Eaux-Vives at Geneva. The grounds were the former residence of one of the promoters of the Gotthard Tunnel. The hilly site posed problems resolved by a fascinating layout of a circle within a circle, with a spectacular tunnel and viaduct. Italian navvies did most of the spade work, 'managing the work with conspicuous success'! The line opened in July 1912 and passengers were conveyed in Bassett-Lowke open coaches with 'Luna Park Express' in brass letters – 'gold plated to prevent tarnishing' on the sides and

Geneva 1912. The 'Luna Park Express' hauled by No 19 *Hungaria* runs into the main station. To the left work is in progress for a second line through the station and in the background is one of the renowned 'rustic' overbridges. (*John Harrison*)

awnings fitted 'during the hot weather'. The fare was 30 centimes for adults, 20 for children. At that time £1 was equivalent to 25 Swiss Francs with 100 centimes to 1 Franc. 'The finest 15in Miniature Railway in the World' (*Models, Railways and Locomotives* July 1912) did, however, leave an interesting poser for today's enthusiast. It was intended that a new Class 30 Atlantic should work the line. However, John Wills' photograph album shows a Class 10 on the first train across the viaduct. It seems that No 19 *Hungaria* was holding the fort until the Class 30 *Sans Pareil* was completed. Before this the park went bankrupt and the bailiffs were due. One night, forewarned, John Wills, as operating manager, spirited away the locomotive, coaches and station clock by horse dray across the border to avoid seizure. *Hungaria* later ran on a line in Angol Park, Budapest, surviving two world wars and countless political crises until the present day.

Narrow Gauge Railways Ltd was at a final exhibition in 1914 at Oslo, ironically to celebrate 100 years of peace since the Congress of Vienna. *Sans Pareil*, now renamed *Prins Olaf*, was dispatched with the Geneva coaches. However, the operating season was brought to an end with the outbreak of war. The driver, William Vaughan, had great difficulty organising the transport of the stock home and did not reach England until August 1915. He found Narrow Gauge Railways Ltd in the midst of its largest venture yet.

CHAPTER FIVE

'FROM FELLS TO COAST'

Narrow Gauge Railways at Ravenglass and Fairbourne

In forming Narrow Gauge Railways Ltd Bassett-Lowke and Proctor-Mitchell had a new concept of longer minimum gauge lines in mind. As early as March 1912 *Models, Railways and Locomotives* carried an advertisement:

> Wanted – Suitable sites for 15 inch gauge Miniature Railways . . . either a mile circuit or a two or three mile run between places of interest is required.

They faced great difficulties in working through conventional channels but John Wills searched assiduously and found another way. He discovered two sites in glorious scenery on the West Coast of Britain where existing tracks lay derelict and were suitable for conversion to 15in gauge.

The Ravenglass & Eskdale Railway proved to be Narrow Gauge Railways' greatest achievement. 'Ratty' as the line is still affectionately known, began life in 1875 as a 3ft gauge line

Muncaster Mill in September 1915. Sans Pareil stands with the Geneva and Oslo coaches now appropriately labelled 'Eskdale Express'. (John Harrison)

running from the Furness Railway at Ravenglass up the valleys of the Rivers Mite and Esk to the village of Boot, nestling under England's highest mountain, Scafell. At Boot were iron ore mines, the line's *raison d'être*, though passengers had also been carried from 1876. The initial hope and prosperity were short lived and the line struggled from crisis to crisis, in the hands of a receiver. Tourists came in greater numbers in the early years of this century, but in spite of further attempts at revival in 1909, the *Cumberland Annual* of 1913 recalled 'The Eskdale Railway closed 30th April 1913'. In June 1915, Bassett-Lowke, Proctor-Mitchell and Wills walked the overgrown trackbed, saw its potential and concluded a lease with Edward Dawson, the major shareholder of the moribund Eskdale Railway Co. Before the lease was signed Wills was masterminding the conversion of the track to 15in gauge using the existing rails on the soundest parts of the old sleepers.

The first mile to Muncaster Mill was ready in six weeks, and 'La'al Ratty', as the line was now known, opened on 28 August 1915. Work continued into the winter, reaching the mid-point by New Year, Eskdale Green by 27 March

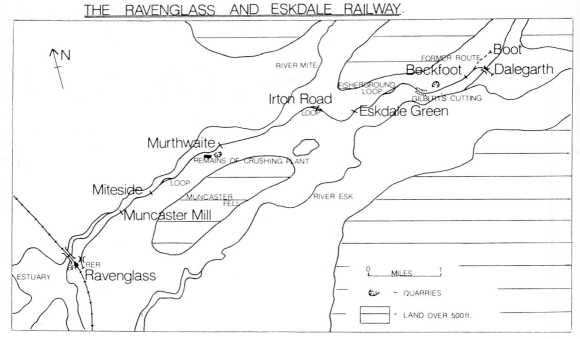

THE RAVENGLASS AND ESKDALE RAILWAY.

and Beckfoot by 20 April 1916. The final mile to Boot up the fearsome 1 in 38 gradient was not opened until August 1917 when the iron ore mines were briefly reopened. Services were cut back to Beckfoot the following year when the mine finally closed. From 1920 the terminus was by the old mine cottages, finally replaced by the present site by the main valley road in 1926.

Rolling stock was a microcosm of minimum gauge thinking. At the opening *Sans Pareil* and seven Bassett-Lowke four-wheel opens arrived from Oslo to join Heywood wagons, a coach and van. In the winter *Katie* was acquired from Eaton Hall to work goods trains, followed before Easter by Howey's Pacific, promptly renamed *Colossus*. After Sir Arthur Heywood's death all his coaches and some wagons quickly arrived, followed in 1917 by the locomotives *Ella* and *Muriel* after their sojourn on military service. The coaches were ideal for the line, the locomotives less so – they ran short of steam and traction, and passengers were frequently required to push trains or pick flowers.

Keith Davies, in his definitive history of the Ravenglass & Eskdale, called these the days of 'the Amateur/Professionals'. In a carefree manner, Proctor-Mitchell managed a staff that included the old personnel, the world's fastest barber and some enthusiastic students, trying to

keep the customers happy when the train had been commandeered for joy riding. The need to run a practical railway service made the line increasingly dependent on the benevolence of Sir Aubrey Brocklebank, of shipping line fame and an early 7¼in gauge enthusiast. In 1919 he sponsored a new slightly more powerful Pacific built by Hunts of Bournemouth, and naturally named *Sir Aubrey Brocklebank*.

By the early 1920s 'Ratty' had made a creditable effort to be a real community railway, and no doubt Heywood would have fully approved. The day to day operations were marvellously recorded by a local photographer, Mary Fair. In the summer season even the goods wagons were swept out to carry the crowds, and from 1920–24 a slip coach service to Irton Road gave connections to charabanc tours to Wasdale. From 1917 to 1928 the Royal Mail for Eskdale demanded a daily service come rain or shine. This gave rise to the 'Scooters', lightweight motor cycle powered contraptions, that roared along the track up and down the valleys at hair raising speeds. Goods traffic grew steadily with coal, coke, cattle feed, farm machinery and general merchandise going up the line. In return, came pit props, sawn timber, potatoes and wool. However, a larger and more staple traffic was required to compensate for the short

(above)
Heywood days at Ravenglass. *Muriel* with complementary carriages leaves Irton Road whilst in the background Scafell dominates the head of Miterdale. (*Mary Fair*)

(below)
June 1923 – a visiting party of railway superintendents in conference at the Furness Abbey Hotel view the newly opened crushing plant at Murthwaite. The locomotives are the Pacifics, *Colossus* and *Sir Aubrey Brocklebank* and talking to the driver of the former is Robert Proctor-Mitchell. (*Mrs E H Steel*)

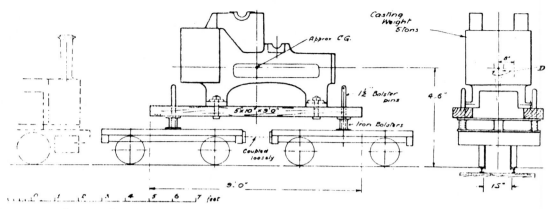

An exceptional load: five tons being carried on the 15in gauge railway at Eskdale in 1923.

tourist season. In 1922, Sir Aubrey Brocklebank supported a local co-operative to reopen the Beckfoot granite quarry alongside the track. To process the granite a crushing plant was built at an isolated spot 2½ miles from Ravenglass at Murthwaite. The plant was laid out in a massive concrete structure reinforced by old rails, designed by the new consulting engineer, a stalwart Narrow Gauge Railways man – Henry Greenly. The layout and operation of the plant

Ravenglass in 1925 showing *River Esk* in original form. *Muriel* is in the background with an extra train made up of Heywood open wagons fitted with temporary seats. (*Mary Fair*)

was not completely satisfactory and it was altered in 1928, though the original concrete still stands.

To haul stone from the quarries and to cope more easily with passenger traffic, Greenly designed the elegant *River Esk*, twice as powerful as the existing locomotives – the first 2-8-2 in this country. Greenly was convinced of the advantages of overscale boiler and working parts and masked a narrow gauge engine inside a one-third scale outline. The builders, Davey, Paxman & Co of Colchester, fitted its patent valve gear to work Lentz poppet valves but this was replaced by Walschaerts gear in 1928 when the locomotive briefly ran with a steam powered Poultney tender.

By 1924 Sir Aubrey had acquired a controlling interest in the railway and the freehold of the site. The following year Proctor-Mitchell and Bassett-Lowke resigned their directorships, and as a share in the operation was held by fellow shipping magnate, Henry Lithgow, the company offices moved to the Cunard Building at Liverpool's Pier Head. Another locomotive trial was held at Ravenglass at this time when Captain Howey's new *Green Goddess* was steamed. Another one-third scale Greenly design built by Davey Paxman, *Green Goddess* was a Pacific based on the *Flying Scotsman*. The machine was a great success and Howey even offered to buy the railway as he had no line of his own. Proposals for an extension over the mountain passes of Hardknott and Wrynose to Ambleside were dreamed of, but Sir Aubrey refused to sell.

The need for new motive power was clear in spite of *River Esk* and a Ford 'Model T' powered machine. *Katie* had gone to Southport by 1920,

but her sisters needed new boilers. *Ella* was altered to take a car engine, *Muriel* to take a conventional locomotive type boiler, emerging in 1927 as *River Irt* and still running today on Heywood's chassis. *Sans Pareil* was scrapped, totally worn out, providing spare parts for the scale Pacifics, which were amalgamated in 1928 to form a 4-6-6-4 *River Mite*. More internal combustion locomotives came from Muir Hill for the granite traffic. This eventually grew to 30,000 tons a year and it was considered viable to construct a standard gauge line from Ravenglass to Murthwaite to avoid transhipping. A standard gauge shunter from Kerr Stuart arrived in 1929 to work the granite ballast which was destined largely for the trackbeds of the LMS.

The direct control of Sir Aubrey Brocklebank saw a progressive improvement of the whole railway from the track upwards. It was even possible to sip tea from the railway's own marked china in the cafe at Dalegarth. From Sir Aubrey's death in 1929, investment was restricted and the Depression bit hard into traffic, though the railway and quarry kept full employment in the district. The mails were lost to the road from 1928 and the daily trains stopped.

The seaward end of the Fairbourne Railway emphasising the sandy environment. In the summer of 1916 *Prince Edward of Wales* heads inland with a light train. (*John Snell*)

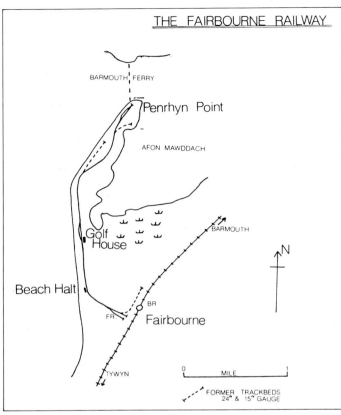

The summer season passenger traffic was discontinued for the duration of the second world
war in September 1939, though granite traffic
continued in full swing with internal combustion
engined locomotives. *River Esk* and *River Irt*
were quietly stored to await better times.

The other Narrow Gauge Railways Ltd line
was at Fairbourne, a small resort south of the
Mawddach estuary in Merioneth. In 1890
Mr Arthur McDougall, later of self-raising flour
fame, began to develop the area and laid a
2ft 0in gauge tramway to move bricks and building materials. It was extended to Penrhyn Point
to connect with the Barmouth Ferry and with
two horse-drawn trams became a tourist attraction. John Wills took over the two-mile line in
1916 and converted it to 15in gauge with a new
terminus by the Cambrian Railways' level crossing. This had a run-round, signal box and shed.
The track followed Beach Road for half a mile
before turning into the sand dunes.

Original motive power was Class 20 Atlantic
Prince Edward of Wales, resplendent in green
edged in maroon probably completed before the

Bassett-Lowke works was fully involved with
the war effort. Five standard four-wheel coaches
were red with black iron work. By 1918 the
locomotive needed major repairs and on its
return from the makers, John Wills became local
manager, remaining after NGR relinquished
its lease until his retirement in 1935. In June
1923 *Katie* arrived from Southport as spare locomotive but by now completely worn out, and
with the reputation of the black sheep of the
Minimum Gauge world. The line had been
leased by the Barmouth Motor Boat and Ferry
Co – a group of ex-servicemen – in 1922. They
could not keep up with the payments on *Prince
Edward of Wales* and it was sold to Llewelyn at
Southport after the 1923 season. Two wet
summers, financial irregularities and *Katie's*
distressing habits defeated them and in 1925 the
line was run by the leasors, the Fairbourne
Estate and Development Co. They used a
virtually new Bassett-Lowke Class 30 which
arrived marked HR. It had been completed in
the previous year for Count Louis Zborowski's
private line at Higham near Canterbury.

New motive power on the Fairbourne in 1925. The Class 30 Atlantic, later *Count Louis*, leaves the main station alonside Beach Road. Note the initials 'H.R.', Highams Railway, on the tender. (*Derek Brough*)

Zborowski was a motor racing and miniature railway enthusiast who, until his death in the Italian Grand Prix at Monza in October 1924, was a friend of Captain Howey.

To the second world war, *Count Louis*, as Wills named the Class 30, was the mainstay of the line.

> The little line runs from Fairbourne Station to the shore, then through the sand dunes and past the golf course to Penrhyn Point . . . the train is hauled by a miniature Atlantic locomotive . . . cars are few or many according to traffic requirements . . .

said a local guide of 1928 when the fare was 6d.

Katie had been dismantled in 1926 leaving the frames as a coach with a wonderful habit of catching passengers' ankles with the crankpins! There was another spare locomotive, a 4-2-2 model of a Stirling 8ft 'Single' built from parts supplied by Bagnall and completed in 1898 by students at the Regent Street Polytechnic; Greenly had marked out the expansion links. One problem was that it was 18in gauge and slowly a length of track was made dual gauge but the locomotive only travelled the full distance a handful of times. Proposals to convert the 'Single' to a 15in gauge 0-6-0 came to naught and it was sold to the Jaywick Railway in 1935. A more practical spare locomotive arrived in that year, a petrol engined Lister which could be used for first and last trains. In the last year of peace, the staff went to look at the Southend stock, wanting to buy *Synolda*. At the end of 1939 *Count Louis* broke a connecting rod but the Lister carried on until the line closed in the summer of 1940.

CHAPTER SIX
'MULTUM IN PARVO'
The Romney, Hythe & Dymchurch Light Railway

John Edwards Presgrave Howey was heir to a fortune, based on the ownership of part of the city centre of Melbourne. This enabled him to follow his interest in small railways culminating in 1914 with the purchase of Bassett-Lowke Pacific *John Anthony* for Staughton Manor. He sold this locomotive to the Narrow Gauge Railways Ltd at Ravenglass in 1916, as he was, at the time, a downed Royal Flying Corps observer and prisoner of war. After the war, now Captain Howey, he raced fast boats and cars, meeting Count Louis Zborowski in 1921 at Brooklands. This Polish/American had a vision of a 15in gauge miniature main line railway with double track and the fastest scale locomotives possible. By 1924, Zborowski had started his own estate railway at Higham with the last Bassett-Lowke Class 30, but in June he visited Eskdale with Howey to see *River Esk* and to meet Henry Greenly.

Greenly produced specifications for one-third scale Pacific locomotives and took charge of their design and construction at Davey, Paxman at Colchester. Two ordered by Zborowski, were to be completed within six months. This and the choice of the Gresley Great Northern prototype ties in with a 15in gauge line 'that, in spite of Mr Greenly's own surveying and planning efforts, did not mature at Wembley' for the 1925 British Empire Exhibition. However, all work stopped after Zborowski's death racing at Monza in October 1924. He left the first locomotive to Howey and it was completed as *Green Goddess* for trials at Ravenglass in June 1925. Encouraged by his mother, who felt any interest was better than racing cars, Howey was to turn his friend's dreams of a miniature main line into reality, and engaged Greenly as his engineering mentor.

It was not easy to find a site that could be developed. The Eskdale line was not for sale, nor was the Hundred of Manhood and Selsey Tramway available for conversion. A line surveyed from Weston-super-Mare to Burnham

could not receive a Light Railway Order against Great Western Railway opposition. In contrast the Southern Railway's General Manager actually suggested to Greenly the holiday area at Dymchurch which could be linked to the SR's existing railheads at New Romney and Hythe. The SR's constituent South Eastern Railway had obtained powers for a link in 1884, but a full size line was now unlikely. Howey proposed to build the new railway at his own cost to feed traffic onto the standard gauge.

Greenly found the flat land of Romney Marsh ideal for the purpose, with only small drainage channels to bridge. In September Howey gave orders to proceed; in October surveying began and the second Zborowski locomotive was

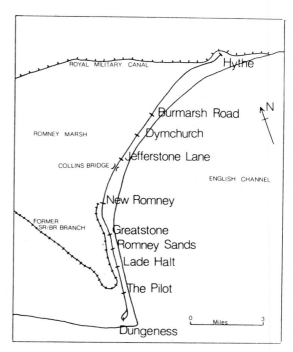

THE ROMNEY, HYTHE AND
DYMCHURCH RAILWAY.

acquired; in November another Pacific was ordered and a formal Light Railway Order was applied for; by December track was laid at the site of New Romney Station. The concept grew from single to half, then full double track. Two main roads required over-bridges but others would have level crossings. At the public inquiry of 15 January 1926, the East Kent Road Car Co objected vigorously but Order 2741 was soon passed forming the Romney, Hythe & Dymchurch Light Railway Co. Railway No 1 was 8 miles 2 furlongs of 15in gauge from opposite New Romney (SR) in a general NE direction to Gallows Corner, Hythe. Railway No 3 was a standard gauge siding across the road at New Romney limited to 4 shunts daily.

New Romney Station was largely complete and there were isolated lengths of track on land already owned, when the LRO was confirmed on 26 May 1926. Everything from the poured concrete structures to the interlocking was designed by Greenly. One exception was the Krauss 0-4-0 tender tank *The Bug* delivered for construction work. Two 4-8-2 mixed traffic locomotives and two three-cylinder Pacifics similar in outline to the other locomotives were ordered from Davey, Paxman. There was a rush to complete the Warren overbridge and the largest sewer bridge for a royal first train, to the certain horror of the railway inspectorate at the

Construction at New Romney as *The Bug* is watered. In the background can be seen the locomotive shed while to the right rise the rafters of 'Red Tiles', Capt Howey's house – now a convalescent home. (*Rick Eyles collection, courtesy National Railway Museum*)

Ministry of Transport. The Duke of York, later King George VI, visited the boys' camp at St Mary's Bay on 6 August 1926 and travelled to New Romney by 15in gauge train. With Howey on the footplate and Mr Gresley perched on the tender, the Duke drove *Northern Chief* back to the camp.

The line was just sufficiently complete for inspection by Lt Col Mount on 25 June 1927. He noted difficulties with bridge foundations, especially at the Willop, though the concrete work was tied into the foundation with rails but showed no sign of settlement – yet! Deflection tests with two trains at 15mph gave ¼in movement. Fully interlocked facing points were required although generally signalling was adequate. A connection into a ballast quarry at milepost 1 was to be removed, and two sidings at Holiday Camp station at Jefferstone Lane needed trap points. Hythe was incomplete and block telephones were to be finished before operation began. 'All were to be congratulated on this unique and interesting undertaking'. It had cost some £110,000, three times the estimate, or about £3 million at current prices!

The line was formally opened on 16 July 1927 by Earl Beauchamp, Lord Warden of the Cinque Ports, who hailed it as 'the most sporting railway in the world' and Howey as 'a fairy with a magic wand'! Locomotive No 5, the unnamed *Hercules* 4-8-2, hauled the 20-coach inaugural train. Within days 4-8-2 *Samson* and 4-6-2 *Hurricane* joined Pacifics *Green Goddess*, *Northern Chief*, *Southern Maid* and *Typhoon* working the 20 daily trains from 6.30am to 9.20pm. 'Conveyances meet all trains at Hythe

Green Goddess leaves Hythe with a train of four-wheeled stock. The ballast reflects the newness of the 'main-line in miniature'. (*Courtesy National Railway Museum*)

for Sandling Junction'. Fares were 10d single from New Romney to Hythe and to Dymchurch 5d, with cheap day returns and season tickets available. In the first 12 weeks, 200,000 passengers were carried and it was decided to extend from New Romney to Dungeness. By October work was underway 'hell for leather' on the five-mile track, and tunnel under the road at New Romney. Services to the Pilot began in

Dymchurch station circa 1930. Greenly's cunning design for the footbridge includes a second use, as indicated by the sign propped against the centre pier! (*Rick Eyles collection, courtesy National Railway Museum*)

May 1928 shortly after the application for an extension Light Railway Order and before an inquiry. Here a temporary triangle for turning locomotives was laid which can still be traced. By August the double line was complete to Dungeness where it formed a large loop with a 600ft platform to take an arriving and departing train together. Lt Col Mount actually inspected and passed the line on 8 September 1928, noting work was needed 'to fit the track for more than 15mph.'

To supplement the original 62 four-wheel vehicles, came another 60-four wheel summer coaches and eight bogie winter coaches with electric lighting and steam heating. A Ford T petrol locomotive of 1928 proved useful if slow, and was completely eclipsed by Howey's 1931 conversion of his Rolls Royce shooting brake.

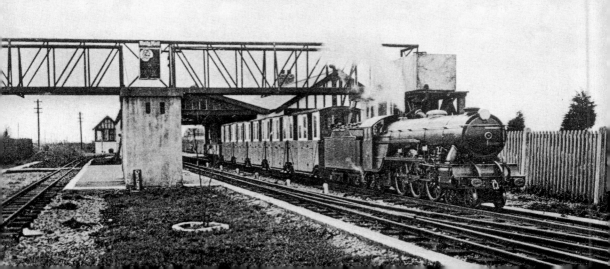

This achieved phenomenal speeds and by 1933 worked the winter services alone. However, two locomotives had been under construction since 1928 with a proposed Canadian outline to protect the driver in winter running. Greenly resigned in a disagreement over them in 1929, so Howey had the parts assembled by the Yorkshire Engine Co to emerge in 1931 as *Dr Syn* and *Black Prince*. Left to run his own railway, Howey improved track layouts for ease of working as operations had not gone as Greenly intended and Hythe was the main source of traffic. Many of Greenly's sharp curves built in for visual effect were removed. By 1935 the freight transfer facilities at New Romney were being removed after handling a disappointing average of only 300 tons a year. Much of this had been to supply materials for War Department experimental aircraft sound detectors, via a short branch near Maddieson's Camp. Later shingle ballast was carried from the branch to an unloading ramp at Hythe, using bogie hopper wagons obtained from the R&ER. This prompted the revival of *Hercules* in 1936, after its retirement with *Samson* following the arrival of the new Canadian type locomotives in 1931.

Howey drove his regular locomotive *Hurricane*, and ruled an enthusiastic band of 'slave drivers' with his seven commandments: from 'Thou shalt not emit smoke' to '. . . not run over any sheep'. Summer traffic was hectic and required six locomotives in steam to haul eleven through trains between Hythe and Dungeness, and additional shuttles between Hythe and Dymchurch. Passenger comfort was enhanced by the introduction of 54 new bogie coaches to replace the originals, still poor riding in spite of articulation in sets of five and nine. In 1938 a set of 10 new coaches formed 'The Blue Train' to run a limited stop service to Dungeness in 50min.

The line had become a national institution, a byword in an Alfred Hitchcock film script, although one remarkable event never made the newsreels. Howey had challenged Henry Segrave, holder of the land speed record, to a locomotive race! The timetable was suspended one day for them to race neck and neck from Hythe to New Romney on *Hurricane* and *Typhoon*!

The unique armoured train at Dymchurch in 1940. The former Ravenglass bogie hopper wagons each mount two Lewis guns and an anti-tank rifle, while in the centre *Hercules* is swathed in a cocoon of armour-plating. (*Imperial War Museum*)

Even in wartime the line operated until the civilian population was evacuated. In June 1940 after Dunkirk, it was requisitioned by Major Beath of the Somerset Light Infantry who found enough railwaymen in his battalion to run troop trains and laundry specials. *Hercules* and two bogie hopper wagons were fitted at Ashford Works with armour plating, four Lewis guns and two anti tank rifles. The 'armoured train' was kept in steam at all times, living under a camouflaged hill on a siding near Dymchurch. The train was allowed to penetrate the barbed wire defences along Dungeness Beach, and even claimed to have shot down a Dornier in retaliation for the repeated bomb damage to the line. Other military units misused the line until it was taken over by the Royal Engineers under the command of Col Kenneth Cantlie. A five locomotive service ran at weekends with tickets bearing the legend 'Romney, Hythe & Dymchurch Military (Light) Railway' for 6d return. During winter 1943–4 the line handled part of the construction of the land end of PLUTO (Pipe Line Under The Ocean). Pipes welded into 300ft lengths at New Romney were taken to Lade by train, later being dragged by crawler along the trackbed doing untold damage to rails and sleepers. Latterly the whole line was disused but it remained in a military zone until July 1945, when Capt Howey was able to repossess his wrecked property.

CHAPTER SEVEN

BRANCH LINES
Other Developments in the Inter War Years

Romney and Ravenglass with their emphasis on passenger carrying were the Minimum Gauge main lines. One branch line tried to develop Heywood doctrines on agricultural light railways so that 'the farmers' interests will be served to the best possible advantage and the country roads and byways kept safe for light motor cars, horse drawn traffic, bicyclists and pedestrians'. Sir Robert Walker returned from the Great War with plans to expand the Sand Hutton Railway to serve his tenant farmers. A Light Railway Order was proposed in November 1919 for 7¼ miles of 15in gauge track from Warthill on the North Eastern Railway, through Sand Hutton to the village of Scrayingham. The River Derwent would be crossed by a large bridge costed at £2052. With branches to outlying farms, the total cost was estimated at £23,271 to be funded by the estate trustees. The Order was confirmed in May 1920 and three miles of track laid from Warthill to Sand Hutton that year. Greenly was involved in the design of more suitable locomotives and rolling stock than *Synolda* used on construction work. However in December 1920,

the 18in gauge rolling stock from Deptford Meat Market became available. Sir Robert snapped this up and the line was regauged and extended. The 15in stock was dispersed but the 18in line had a butterfly existence, fluttering through the 1920s before closing in 1932 after the death of its sponsor. Even in the same month as the LRO application the local National Farmers' Union had started to organise lorry transport direct from the farm to market, so that the line was doomed at birth. *The Locomotive Magazine* later commented:

> Worked by miniature rolling stock it might have taken its place with the Ravenglass & Eskdale and Romney, Hythe & Dymchurch as a popular holiday line. Petrol engined locomotives . . . could have provided the motive power for all but the trains for holiday traffic thereby reducing the number of scale steam locomotives.

Synolda actually vanished into a maelstrom of miniature railway wheeling and dealing where

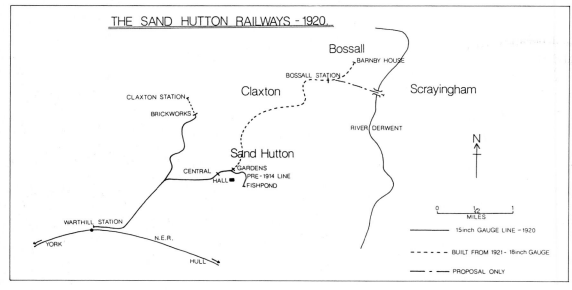

LAKESIDE MINIATURE RAILWAY, SOUTHPORT
G7051

(*above*)
A busy day on the Lakeside Miniature Railway at Southport in the early 1930s. In the foreground *King George V* formerly *Prince Edward of Wales* (Fairbourne) enters the station with a train. (*John Harrison*)

(*below*)
The second station at Rhyl is evident in this July 1934 postcard. The locomotives are 'Albion' class Atlantics, *Joan* and *Michael*. (*Simon Townsend Collection*)

MINIATURE RAILWAY STATION, MARINE LAKE, RHYL.
218926

old lines and new acquired locomotives from each other, often changing their names, to the confusion of enthusiasts. At Southport the Lakeside station was extended with two tracks in 1919, before the arrival of *Katie* from Ravenglass and *Mighty Atom* from Sutton Park, both in poor condition. The latter was overhauled in 1920 taking the name of the existing Class 20 *Prince of Wales* that was now running as *G V Llewelyn* and later as *Lloyd George*! With the arrival of *Prince Edward of Wales* from Fairbourne in late 1923, Southport naming policy lost all reason and this locomotive was noted as *Sir Albert Stephenson* on one side and *King George V* on the other! Llewelyn became totally dependent on Harry Barlow for maintenance and he took over the leases in 1933. *Prince of Wales* had already been sold in 1929 to Yarmouth and there was not a complete locomotive on site. Barlow rescued one and rebuilt the other Class 20, naming them *Princess Elizabeth* and *King George V*. He had just secured a long lease after some uncertainty when in 1938 a fire destroyed the workshops with the locomotives inside. It was reputedly caused by the shorting of batteries being charged for the evening

The ultra-modern image of 1934 is reflected in this view of Park Station on the Dreamland Miniature Railway, Margate. Both trains are composed of Bassett-Lowke open coaches. *Billie* leads the one on the right with *Prince Edward of Wales* nearer the camera. (*Royal Commission on Historical Monuments [England]*)

running of the *Glass Coach* as the saloon was known. Both engines required substantial rebuilding to run again.

At Rhyl the station was also extended in 1919 with a magnificent wooden overall roof. In this 'Victory Season' the Class 10 Atlantics ran from 10am to 10pm daily! Such intense running re-emphasised the shortcomings of their narrow fireboxes and the need for bigger engines. Construction began on the batch of six Albion Class 4-4-2s designed by Greenly to be built in the Albion Works of Albert Barnes. No 101 *Joan* was completed for August Monday 1920 and had allowed the sale of *Prince Edward of Wales* to a new line at Margate in May. By April 1921, Barnes had completed the third Albion, allowing the sale of the second Class 10 *George the Fifth* to a line at Skegness. The third and fourth Albions were sold, but the final two, *Michael* and *Billy*, were not finished until the early 1930s to run at Rhyl.

Greenly had designed the Dreamland Miniature Railway at Margate completely and supervised its construction in four months – a record time considering the 600yd circuit, five span 86ft viaduct and various concrete buildings. 'At one stage there were three gangs working on the bridge piers, the wooden girders and the track . . . all in friendly rivalry' wrote Greenly. In 1924 the track was altered to give an out and back run from a terminus with a traverser. By 1927 another Albion class *Billie* had come to join *Prince Edward of Wales* and the 1911 vintage Bassett-Lowke coaches, all of which were to run there until 1980.

George the Fifth was in operation at Skegness by 1922. The track ran on the sea side of North Parade from the Pier to the figure-of-eight switchback ride at Pleasureland. Here was a balloon loop and open fronted stock shed. However the locomotive was soon in such poor condition that it was running with 2ft of stovepipe in the chimney to aid steaming! The lease, held by a Mr Bond was terminated in 1928 when Pleasureland was relocated, and the stock went to join the Hershell Spillman 4-4-0 at Southend.

More locomotive perambulations led another Albion class *Michael* to the quarter mile long Woodland Park Miniature Railway in Cuckold's Woods on the banks of the Medway at Rochester by 1923. Early in 1926 it arrived at the Saracen's Head Pub between Healey and Warburton in

The return of a Cagney to Scotland. This 1936 view of the Ettrick Bay Railway shows an immaculate *Samson* with Driver McQueen at the regulator. The 'tunnel' is evident in the background as are the roadside power poles of the Rothesay Tramways – the owners of the railway. (*Rick Eyles collection, courtesy National Railway Museum*)

George the Fifth is fitted with a chimney extension to aid steaming in this 1926 postcard of the Skegness Miniature Railway. (*H. Wilkinson Collection*)

Cheshire, after the publican George V Tonner had apparently acquired it in Blackpool. Renamed *George V Junior* running was curtailed in 1928 when a valuable racehorse broke its fetlock tripping over the rails of the circuit! The railway was sold to Belle Vue Zoo at Manchester and a 200yd straight was opened for Easter 1929. The locomotive soon became *Railway Queen* to participate in the annual rally of railway trades unions at which the Railway Queen personality girl was elected. The track was extended into a 500yd loop with a tunnel-cum-stock shed. In 1938 the Class 10 *George the Fifth* arrived from Southend followed in the middle of the second

world war by *Synolda* and a petrol electric railcar via Dunn's of Bishop Auckland.

Little Elephant, the original *Little Giant*, had been rebuilt by Bassett-Lowke in 1923; after some 100,000 miles 'very little of the original engine is left so far as the working parts are concerned'. It went to another line at Halifax, the Sunny Vale Miniature Railway owned by a Mr Bunce, and was dubiously renamed *Baby Bunce*! Only 200 yd long, the line was graced by scale model dummy passengers and lasted until 1953.

Prince of Wales, alias *Mighty Atom*, was sold in 1929 to Nigel Parkinson's Yarmouth Miniature Railway, still bearing Llewelyn's Miniature Railway on the tender sides. Parkinson had earlier built a 14in gauge three-rail electric railcar for his garden line at Sheringham, but realised the advantages of the Minimum Gauge for commercial operation as stock could be obtained readily. Opened for August 1930 the line was entirely reconstructed for the following season. In this form a balloon loop of 530yd led out of South Denes Junction, a station with two island platforms. Bridging the tracks was the booking office and waiting room with a vaulted roof 'a copy of that at St Pancras though the span is 10ft not 240'! Beyond was a turntable, typical of Parkinson's attention to details of operation that a mere showman would ignore. All the tracks were fully signalled, remotely worked from a box on the bridge over the platforms. The Class 10 was rebuilt with an outside framed trailing truck and smoke deflectors. Other stock built by Parkinson included a petrol locomotive based on a North Eastern Railway electric, eight scale four-wheel wagons with seats, and three saloon carriages. Two similar vehicles formed a petrol-electric railcar set.

Parkinson also took over the line of W. H. Bond at Woodgrange Drive, Southend, in 1932. He extended it down a 1 in 60 gradient through deep clay cuttings and a 60yd tunnel to a new station. This Central station had a single platform under a trainshed of the same structure used at Yarmouth. To work the line came *George the Fifth* from Skegness, and *Synolda* which had spent the years since leaving Sand Hutton in obscurity. Parkinson built a crude steam outline petrol locomotive, and converted the Skegness coaches into an articulated set with roofs. Dwarfed by the Bassett-Lowke locomotives was the line's ancient Herschell Spillman 4-4-0 which had lost its cowcatcher and gained some inelegant boiler cladding. When the line closed in 1938, the rolling stock went north.

The main line atmosphere is reflected in this picture of the Yarmouth Miniature Railway. The coaches are complete with 'corridor ends' and the elaborate station with elevated signalbox is only let down by the grassy permanent way. *Prince of Wales*, formerly *Mighty Atom*, seems overwhelmed by its smoke deflectors. (*Real Photographs, courtesy Ian Allan Ltd*)

Admiring crowds in Belfast for a purely Romney train; *The Bug* alias *Jean* leaves Belle Hazel with a train of four-wheeled coaches. (*Rick Eyles Collection, courtesy of National Railway Museum*)

On the closure of the Yarmouth line in 1937, *Prince of Wales* returned to its original home at Sutton Park with the petrol electric locomotive and the saloon coaches. The original track from Crystal Palace to Windley Pool had last been used in 1921–3, and this was incorporated into a new balloon loop layout by Parkinson for the Midlands showman Pat Collins. *Prince of Wales* operated throughout the war but the petrol electric succumbed to rationing in 1943.

The petrol locomotive gained in popularity in the 1930s; indeed one line laid in 1932 has used no other. This stretched from Salt Lake to Coney Beach at Porthcawl, 440yd with a passing loop and tunnel/stock shed. The first locomotive *Coney Queen* was locally built using the fin controls of an old submarine, though following the construction of *Silver Jubilee* in 1935, both machines had electric drive from Tilling Stevens buses. The 12 coaches were redundant four wheelers from the Romney, Hythe & Dymchurch, five never having seen service there.

Other surplus Romney stock included *The Bug* and six original coaches that formed the improbable *Honeymoon Express* run by Harry Kamiya in Blackpool in 1933. The next year they were sold to Belfast Corporation and taken from the docks to Belle Vue Park by horse dray. Here the track ran from Belle Vue to Bell Hazel with very tight balloon loops at both ends. *The Bug* was renamed *Sir Crawford* after Lord Mayor Sir Crawford McCullagh, but this was too formal for the locals who soon shortened it to *Jean*. After the line closed in 1959 the locomotive survived under a pile of scrap in Andersonstown to be rescued and returned to New Romney in 1972.

Another locomotive of foreign construction was a Cagney 4-4-0 reported running at Cleethorpes during the 1920s. This ran behind the amusements at Wonderland, and had links with another local miniature railway. It seems likely that this was the Blakesley locomotive, the one sold in 1932 to a Mr Sword for his youngest son. Sword was a director of Rothesay Tramway Co on the Isle of Bute. The locomotive now named *Samson* was used on a circle of track by the Ettrick Bay tram terminus, from 1936 until 1943. Later in 1946–8 it ran at Millport on Great Cumbrae island.

Private 15in gauge railways were rare; The

Hardwicke Manor Railway had its origins in a set of castings for a Bassett-Lowke Class 30 Atlantic purchased before the first world war. Afterwards work continued and the locomotive was completed in 1933 in spite of the loss of the original drawings. Named *Douglas Clayton*, after its owner who was a director of Carron Iron-foundries, it ran with three bogie open coaches and a magnificent bogie compartment coach, complete with window straps, leather seats, real photographs and electric lights. A second locomotive to the same design was started in 1938 but war, then the death of the owner postponed completion.

Some proposed schemes did not turn out as they might. The North Bay Railway at Scarborough was to have been a 15in gauge line and Bassett-Lowke was invited to tender, apparently to build 2-6-4 tanks similar to Greenly's proposal for Sand Hutton. In the event the line was 20in gauge equipped by Hudswell Clarke with diesel-engined Gresley style Pacifics in 1931. In 1933 Southport Council advertised for a contractor/operator to replace the 15in gauge line with a 20in gauge. The scheme came to naught and the Lakeside Railway flourished under Harry Barlow's hands instead.

This failure of Bassett-Lowke in the field of 15in gauge was reflected in the international exhibitions of the inter-war period, which were usually supplied with German 15in equipment. For the 1925 Munich Transport Exhibition, Krauss München AG had laid a mile long circuit with a triangular junction to its main terminus. This and the Sud station had separate arrival and departure platforms to obviate much of the

trouble experienced on other lines during 'rush hours'. To work the line with its 196ft tunnel and 1 in 50 ruling gradient, came three one-third scale Class K3/6 Pacifics which could haul 10 coach trains of 16 seat opens. Roland Martens, Chief Engineer of Krauss Light Locomotive Department consulted his old friend Henry Greenly over every aspect of the line especially the locomotives. It was a great success, handling over 7000 passengers a day at its peak. The Pacifics were sold the next year and replaced by two 0-4-0WTs similar to *The Bug*. Erich Brangsch, a locomotive dealer of Leipzig, used them at exhibitions at Rotterdam in 1928, Antwerp in 1930 and Cork in 1932. The K3/6 Pacific design was repeated for the Lilliputbahn im Prater at Vienna in 1928 and for a line at Leipzig giving another six locomotives. The following year a batch of four were built for the AEG Ibero-American Exposition in Seville, together with two boilers for the Romney, Hythe & Dymchurch Canadian Pacifics.

When three more locomotives were needed for an exhibition at Dusseldorf in 1937, Krauss München was not in business and the nationalised firm Fried. Krupp built a very similar design, all three examples of which were to come to Britain in the 1970s. However loss of Krupp's records during the war led to the original design being chosen for a locomotive given to the Tata Works in India, and two more were built for Stuttgart in 1950. Of the earlier machines three still run on the Dresden Pioneereisenbahn, two at the Prater Park in Vienna, one in Madrid, with others stored or suffering the ignomony of being converted to diesel power.

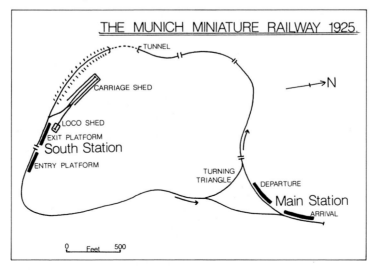

THE MUNICH MINIATURE RAILWAY 1925.

CHAPTER EIGHT

NORMAL SERVICE WILL BE RESUMED
Postwar Developments

After the second world war, no-one had more to do than Capt Howey; the track of the RHDR was overgrown and impassable in the Hythe direction while the Dungeness line had been wrecked by tracked vehicles. Locomotives were worn out while many of the coaches had been stripped of their bodies for the Pluto trains. Under the management of Capt J. T. Holder, prisoners of war cleared the line so that it could be reopened on 1 March 1946 to Hythe and by midsummer to Maddieson's Camp. The latter was now a single track penetrating the barbed wire, but the holiday camps were soon in full swing after six years of war, and the railway was almost overwhelmed. There was also a revival of

A meeting at Dymchurch in 1949. *Hurricane* approaches with a train from Hythe while *Green Goddess* prepares to depart. The unprotected level-crossing looks an unlikely prospect to today's safety-conscious eyes. (*T. J. Edgington*)

ballast traffic with up to four trains, at night if required, from the WD branch through to Hythe where an unloading ramp was built; later ballast was unloaded at New Romney.

The revival pushed the locomotives to the limit, and the Southern Railway was persuaded to allow Ashford works to rebuild four locomotives while further four were done at New Romney and another by an outside contractor. The celebration of the line's 21st Birthday occasioned great junketings on 21 March 1947, when Laurel and Hardy gave their services and made world news! The next decade saw the heyday of passenger carrying as holidaymakers flocked to the Kent Coast. The RHDR carried more passengers than all the other tourist lines put together, and peak services required seven locomotives in steam. New coach bodies were built ranging from rudimentary opens to the streamlined observation cars *Pluto* and *Martello*. The stock was further increased by the Eaton

The Far Tottering & Oystercreek Railway at the Festival of Britain in 1951. The bizarre *Neptune*, modelled on a paddle-steamer, eventually reverted to type as *Prince Charles* at Southport. (*Valentines of Dundee Ltd*)

Railway coaches and Simplex petrol locomotive in 1947. Locomotive working was made easier and more economical by the introduction of new superheated boilers after experiments with *Northern Chief* in 1952. The reboilering at a cost of £450 each was the last major investment that Howey put into the line. He still regretted that he had never taken over the Eskdale line in 1925, and was content that the Romney would

see him out. In 1957, Her Majesty the Queen, the Duke of Edinburgh, Prince Charles and Princess Anne travelled from New Romney to Hythe with George Barlow driving *Hurricane*, the Duke and the children sharing a footplate pass.

Howey did his last spell of driving that year at the age of 70, but kept a close eye on trains from his summerhouse by New Romney signalbox. He died on 8 September 1963 and his ashes lie in the rockery opposite. His railway faced an uncertain future.

It was business as usual at Belle Vue, Rhyl and Southport, which could claim with the Windmill Theatre 'we never closed'. In 1948, the Southport line was extended beyond the pier to Peter Pan's Pool, and both termini had loops

A rural view of the latter years of the Sutton Miniature Railway. *Sutton Belle* hauling the former Yarmouth rail-car seems remote from any commercialisation. (*Peter Julian*)

to allow three train operation. To develop additional motive power Harry Barlow made the purchase of some war surplus searchlight generators, and used two in his petrol-electric 4-6-2 *Duke of Edinburgh*. This was the first of a series resembling A4s that were to travel widely. Another *Duke of Edinburgh* was used at Alexandra Palace, London, from 1950 to 1970, *Princess Anne*, at St Annes from 1956 to 1961, and another on a line at Butlins, Skegness from 1962.

Belle Vue also saw one of these locomotives briefly, on loan when its own steam engine received new boilers. The Class 10 *George the Fifth* however became derelict from the mid 1950s and vanished under the workshop scrap heap. *Railway Queen* and *Prince Charles*, as the one-time *Synolda* was known, were disguised in ignominious Wild West fittings in the 1960s. At this period, Robin Butterell who was researching the history of the Bassett-Lowke locomotives, managed to locate the missing engine and saved it for eventual restoration. By the end in 1977, *Prince Charles* also was derelict and the line was worked by *Railway Queen* and the original Albion class *Joan* from Rhyl.

By far the most bizarre 15in line appeared in 1951 at the Festival of Britain, laid and operated by Harry Barlow. The Far Tottering & Oystercreek Railway was a third of a mile long on the southern edge of the site. The three locomotives were mechanically Barlows but clothed in the designs of Rowland Emett, the cartoonist. *Nellie* was a distinctive saddle tank; *Neptune* had affinities with a paddle steamer, while *Wild Goose* was supposed to be made from a derelict airship! The line lasted in this form to 1953 carrying over 2,000,000 passengers who were cautioned 'Do NOT tease the Engine' and 'Trains cross Here – So There!' Afterwards the track was relaid in Battersea Gardens and operated until 1975 with Barlows of more conventional appearance.

1948 saw yet another reopening at Sutton Coldfield where the line was now under the control of Mr Hunt. In his Oldbury Works, the ageing *Prince of Wales* was given a new firebox and refurbished. Hunt then bought the Hardwicke Manor equipment including the completed Atlantic which was renamed *Sutton Belle* and repainted from green to brown in deference to fairground superstitions! By 1952, the second Hardwicke Manor locomotive was completed

The Twining 2-4-2, later *Katie*, built by Trevor Guest stands outside the locomotive shed at Dudley Zoo in July 1957. Shortly after this photograph was taken the locomotive was purchased by Capt Hewitt and removed to Anglesey. (*Matthew Kerr*)

and named *Sutton Flyer*, allowing the retirement of *Prince of Wales*. Though the line saw the trials of *Dingo* a petrol engined locomotive for the Fairbourne Railway in 1951, it was not until 1957 that a petrol locomotive styled as a Great Western railcar was purchased from Dudley Zoo. The Sutton line prospered, carrying a record 12,000 people on Whit Monday 1960, but, suddenly, it was no more. The lease for the Crystal Palace site in Sutton Park was not to be renewed after 1962 as it was now a policy that the old Sutton Park should not be commercialised. Final closure came on 7 October and within four months the line had gone, leaving a bare trackbed and the stock in store at Oldbury awaiting a new use.

The Dudley Zoo Railway had begun life in 1937 as a 10¼in gauge line laid by Trevor Guest of G. & S. Light Engineering, Stourbridge. In 1946 it was converted to 15in gauge laid on concrete sleepers as an austerity measure. The first locomotive was the GW railcar later sold to Sutton Park. After came a scale outline Stanier Class 5 4-6-0 to a design by Ernest Twining, subsequently named *Prince Charles* and hired to Fairbourne in the early 1960s before being rebuilt as a Pacific. A sister locomotive was altered during construction in 1949 to form *Ernest W. Twining*, a 4-6-2 that ran at Fairbourne

One of the formidable Barlow diesels, *Prince of Wales*, seen beneath the signal gantry on the Saltburn Miniature Railway in August 1965. (*T. J. Edgington*)

for much longer. A further steam locomotive was under construction in 1954 to a narrow gauge 2-4-2 design. As *Katie* it only ran briefly at Dudley Zoo before it was bought by a wealthy eccentric, Capt Hewitt, who intended to use it on a plantation railway in the West Indies. Because of his death it remained stored in Anglesey before being sold to the Fairbourne in 1965. For most of its life the Dudley Zoo line has been worked by diesels built by Guest, one British, another American, and a third *Clara* with a mock steam outline. The track extending out of the Zoo grounds through the woods surrounding the castle rock, is now shortened but still operational.

Closely linked with these lines and Guest was the Fairbourne Railway, revived following wartime damage by storms and military vehicles. In 1946 it had been acquired by three Midlands industrialists and by Easter 1947, trains hauled by the Lister worked as far as the Golf House, while *Count Louis* was rebuilt to work the whole line by the summer. As the line increased in popularity, coaching stock was improved steadily, a passing loop was installed in 1951 and additional trains were worked by the petrol locomotives *Dingo*, *Gwril* and *Whippit Quick*. The original Fairbourne terminus was

very cramped and in 1958, a new station was opened in an adjoining field linked by bridges across an intervening stream. An agricultural type building formed a trainshed over four tracks. Two-aspect colour-light signals were interlocked with facing points and a traverser. To support the early locomotives came the two Guest steam engines followed in 1961 by petrol locomotives *Rachel* and *Sylvia*. The internal combustion fleet at Fairbourne was to keep trains running in the sandy conditions, when even a slight breeze carried dirt into the bearings and motion of a conventional steam locomotive. To combat this a sister of *Katie* was built with these parts protected by oil seals to exclude sand. Completed in 1963 it was named *Sîan* and was joined by the prototype in 1965. After this dramatic development, the line settled down to a period of security that was to last into the 1970s when its owners tried to find a group to succeed them.

The Ravenglass and Eskdale Railway was not devastated by the war but working heavy granite traffic without being able to renew track and stock caused severe problems. With peace a limited summer service with I/C power began, while *River Irt* returned to service in 1947. The death of Henry Lithgow presaged the sale of the line to a quarrying competitor in 1949. The Keswick Granite Co had contracts supplying the new Sellafield plant but realised the competitive potential of Beckfoot, and rather than develop the quarry business closed it in 1953.

The standard gauge line was lifted and the Kerr Stuart diesel sold to Raymond Dunn. However, the new owners promoted the tourist aspect of the line, allowing the completion of a major overhaul to *River Esk* in 1952 and the start of a new diesel incorporating a few small parts of *Ella*. In 1957 a change in the tax law, which stopped the losses of a subsidiary company from being offset against the profits of its parent, suddenly made 'La'al Ratty' a liability to the Keswick Granite Co.

The line was offered for sale in September 1958 as a going concern for £22,500 but no buyer was found. It barely made an operating surplus, let alone enough to cover management costs and urgently needed renewals. Then in 1960, the line was offered for sale by auction with five weeks' notice. An impromptu body of local railwaymen and enthusiasts from all over the country rallied around Douglas Robinson, clerk to the parish council. At the auction on 7 September 1960 in Gosforth Parish Hall the large crowd included scrap merchants and dealers. However, a successful bid (of £12,000) was made by a trust comprising the Preservation Society, Colin Gilbert, a Midlands stockbroker, and Sir Wavell Wakefield. Gilbert as major shareholder became Managing Director until his death in 1968. Continuity was assured when this position was assumed by the now Lord Wakefield of Kendal.

Considerable work was needed to restore track and stock, and policies were established by the new general manager, Douglas Ferreira, that were to be justified over the next 25 years. Some of the track was still the original rail, even the best was Great War military vintage, so since 1965 a short length has been relaid each year with new 35lb rail and Jarrah hardwood sleepers. A major civil engineering project was a new line to bypass a series of sharp reverse curves, via Gilbert's Cutting opened in 1964. Other improvements were made at Ravenglass in 1967 by the complete relaying of the station track, new platforms and the construction of a large carriage shed. The open rolling stock had deteriorated badly but replacement coaches were to include saloons more suited to a Lakeland summer, first the three converted 18in gauge coaches from the Jaywick railway, then in 1967 two prototype aluminium-bodied vehicles. Initially *River Irt* and *River Esk* were given boiler overhauls while the remaining quarry

tractors were refurbished and helped by the arrival of *Royal Anchor* in 1961 for use on light trains. However, a steady growth in traffic encouraged the Preservation Society to sponsor the building of a new *River Mite* on the old Poultney tender chassis. Its dispatch in 1966 from Clarksons at York to Ravenglass by traction engine was a remarkable event that pointed the line to a confident future.

This period also saw developments on some interesting private railways, The Deans Mill Garden Railway is still recorded on a current map of Lindfield in Sussex as a simple circle with tracks into a barn. Its petrol locomotive went to Margate, being rebuilt with a more attractive body. It also had two American switcher types built by Morse, an 0-4-0 of 1939 and an 0-6-0 which went to a line at Potter Heigham before returning in the 1960s to Mr Lemon Burton's extensive private line at Paynesfield in Sussex. The Royal Anchor pub at Liphook saw, in the hands of Charles Lane, probably the largest collection of models and miniature locomotives in the country. It had lines in 10¼in, 15in and 18in gauges in the grounds. *Royal Anchor* was built here before trials on the RHDR in 1957. Stock from another private line also found its way to Romney; this comprised *Redgauntlet* and some genuine former 9½in gauge Heywood wagons built for the early experiments at Dove Leys. During the 1960s

The Fairbourne Railway in July 1969. The line to the right leads into the station while an immaculate *Ernest Twining* comes off the engine shed which until 1958 served as the station. (*T. J. Edgington*)

Still steaming on two days after the auction, *River Irt* stands ready to depart from Ravenglass. Below the running board the locomotive is still substantially *Muriel*. (*T. J. Edgington*)

these vehicles were used on the Jacot Railway around the Jacot family home near Birmingham.

Another privately owned locomotive, the Cagney from Ettrick Bay, was now in the collection of Mr Sword, managing director of Western Scottish Motor Traction, the successors to Rothesay Tramways! It ran on portable lines at events in Central Scotland like the 1958 Castle Douglas Wakes week, before Lord Bruce bought it, hoping to lay a permanent track. It was then sold to Laurence Brooks who restored it and ran it briefly on the RHDR in 1969. It now sadly stands static in Strumpshaw Hall in Norfolk. The other surviving American 4-4-0, the Southend Herschell Spillman, had found its way by 1948 to Seaburn near Sunderland via Younger's Redlands Railroad at Ponteland, and a temporary line on Newcastle's Town Moor. At Seaburn, a new boiler was ordered but it would not fit between the wheels. Though the locomotive was stored in Sunderland Corporation Tram depot, it was eventually scrapped. Its replacement at Seaburn was the 1950 *Royal Scot* 4-6-0 built by Carland Engineering of Harold Wood in Essex. This locomotive was converted in 1960 to diesel using the tender as a radiator, though it is now restored to steam again. The Seaburn line survived until 1981 with an I/C locomotive.

There was a cluster of short lived lines along the Durham coast. These were promoted by the Dunn family at Seaton Carew and Crimdon Dene. In 1948 they opened the Saltburn Miniature Railway with ¾ mile of track from the seafront to the Valley Gardens using the

Yarmouth 2-4-0 petrol locomotive and the veteran *Blacolvesley*. Under new ownership, the line obtained in 1960 the Barlow A4 steam-outline diesel-electric *Prince Charles* from Southport. It ran as *Prince of Wales* until 1976 and is now undergoing restoration by enthusiasts who have saved the partly lifted track.

Another seaside line which grew from a portable track used at fetes was the Voryd Amusement Park Tramway at Rhyl, built in 1951 by Claud Lane, with a quarter mile of overhead electrified route from West Parade to Wellington Road. The popularity of the three scale trams led to the development of another site at Eastbourne from 1954. The gauge this time was 2 feet to give greater stability to double deck trams.

Close by, the Rhyl Miniature Railway still steamed daily around the lake in one of the busiest operations anywhere. Visitors to Rhyl Amusements entered an arcade leading to the station where one of the four locomotives would be waiting as its train loaded. Though the pre-war wooden overall roof was now replaced by concrete, the atmosphere of steam was everywhere. When the other train in service returned, the next one would leave behind the roller-coaster. After a shallow cutting that avoided the worst curve on the original line, trains soon emerged through the sea wall clear of the fairground clutter, running below the Holyhead main line. After a gallop through the trees on the far side of the lake speed fell past the engine shed, enlarged to four roads when rebuilt in brick after the war. With four Albion Class 4-4-2s. *Joan*, *John*, *Michael* and *Billy*, one locomotive in turn received a major overhaul each year, leaving one spare and two in service. Finally the track entered a short 'tunnel' to emerge in the covered station.

CHAPTER NINE

FORWARD TO FIRST PRINCIPLES
Developments to 1985

1968 saw the demise of steam on British Rail; the years since then have seen an unparalleled revival of interest as privately-restored locomotives have returned to the main line and enthusiast groups have resurrected lines for steam operation. Such has been the pattern on the Minimum Gauge, where historic locomotives have been restored, new ones built and new lines opened while historic sites and objects have been secured for the future.

Shortly after Howey's death in 1963 the Romney, Hythe & Dymchurch Railway was taken over by two retired bankers, Messrs Collins and Scatcherd who saw it as a retirement interest. Ignoring the long term little was done to upgrade the track while fresh paint and six inch nails covered a multitude of sins in the coach fleet. Nemesis came when an outside consultant condemned the Duke of York's Bridge and it was replaced in 1968, being completed literally the day before trains were due to run for Easter. A new group of local business men with David Lye as chairman took over in May 1968, fully intending to put the railway to rights. They were dismayed to read the consultant's follow-up report which condemned four other bridges 'largely due to a complete lack of maintenance', but also because of wartime shrapnel damage, and the shifting of the abutments foreseen at the original inspection. The financially brave, if outwardly unspectacular, decision was made to replace the bridges on new deeper foundations. Good rail from the Sierra Leone Government Railway was purchased for repairs to the main line, which previously relied on the remnants of the second Dungeness track. The old workshop building was cleared of curiosities like the complete set of Heywood patterns which arrived from Eaton, and equipped with machine tools to cope with major locomotive repairs. After this *Southern Maid* became the first locomotive to have a major rebuild in seven years, emerging in appropriate Great Northern livery.

However, the need for a considerable future investment confirmed Lye's commercial view that the station sites as building land were worth more than they would ever pay as a railway. Considerable thought was given to ideas of shortening the railway so that it could operate with a reduced amount of stock, and even to moving everything to another site. The simplest solution was that announced in summer 1971 – complete closure. The result was to induce the formation of another consortium, this time linked through the friendship of George Barlow, now the operating manager, and Richard North. In February 1972, the RH&D Light Railway Holding Co Ltd took over the railway under the chairmanship of W. H. McAlpine. Now the object was to 'restore, maintain and develop the railway in line with Howey's and Zborowski's original vision'.

With John Snell as managing director, the railway has gradually recovered. A vast replacement of coaches has taken place with investment in high quality 20 seat vehicles which maintain seating capacity while the actual number of coaches is much reduced. In 1977, the world's largest 15in gauge coach, the Bar Car, was completed, in a gaudy livery sponsored in turn by Courage Breweries, Townsend-Thoresen and presently Camp Coffee. Motive power has been restored by the rebuilding of all the locomotives in turn, mainly by outside contractors, and for several years six locomotives were seen in steam daily at peak times. The original fleet was joined in 1976 by one of the three Krupp Pacifics of 1937, though the name of *Fleissig Lieschen* was altered to *Black Prince*. The line is usually host now to *The Bug*, rescued from Belfast and restored for Bill MacAlpine in 1978. Finally after many years of completely steam operation, trials by two R&ER diesels led to the design and construction of RHDR No 12, *John Southland*, at TMA Engineering of Lichfield. This formidable diesel was completed in 1983.

The need for a diesel resulted from another

The world's largest 15in gauge coach, the RHDR bar car leaves New Romney behind *Northern Chief* in November 1984. (*Peter van Zeller*)

change in the line's fortunes. With a decline in the local holiday market, traffic had not grown back to the heights expected. A public share issue to finance improvements had been disappointing. However, in the Railway's Golden Jubilee Year came a contract from the local authority to run a daily school train from Burmarsh Road and Dymchurch to New Romney. From 1977, in all weathers, it was worked by two steam locomotives, one at each end. Now *John Southland* works push-pull style, and the contract contributes a significant guaranteed income to the railway.

The railway infrastructure continues to improve with steady relaying using second hand materials, and the rationalisation of the station layouts at Hythe and New Romney for simpler operation. Since 1974 the new Maddieson's Camp passing loop has revitalised the operation of the Dungeness line and encouraged more passengers to travel further. Passenger amenities have been improved with a new entrance hall at Hythe and trainshed at New Romney, though

the original Greenly buildings survive to recall the halcyon 1920s. One modern touch is the introduction of automatic flashing lights to full Ministry specifications at all road crossings as the inevitable growth in road traffic has brought a number of collisions between trains and cars.

The level of investment and local authority support has quietened the thoughts of moving to another site in a developing tourist area. However the line now seeks to utilise fully idle rolling stock in schemes such as exhibitions thus returning full circle to its origins. It hoped to be 'operating agents' of a four mile line from Thamesmead sponsored by the Greater London Council. In 1984 the RHDR gave considerable assistance to the International Garden Festival Railway at Liverpool, and followed this by sending *Black Prince* to Japan. In 1985 this locomotive ran in a caravan of British locomotive history that toured from Hiroshima. Such events support the unique miniature main line concept.

It is unlikely that anyone could repeat the RHDR in today's world, and the real sadness is that suburban sprawl and the atomic power station complex have driven away forever the essential wildness of Romney Marsh.

In contrast 'La'al Ratty' has enjoyed a secure

existence and still benefits from the scenery that enchanted the original operators of 1915. The isolation that restricted it for so long has become less important to a car owning public. The policy of relaying the line with new materials has continued and virtually all the main line has been completed, giving a track second to none. Traffic has grown, and to increase capacity two additional passing loops were installed for 1976 at Miteside (1¾ miles from Ravenglass) and Fisherground (5½ miles) enabling a 20-minute headway service to be run if required. Up the line Eskdale Green station was built anew by members of the Preservation Society, Irton Road remains in the state of 1876, and the old gunrange hut at Eskdale (Dalegarth) still stands, though now cedar clad. At Ravenglass, however, there have been great changes with new and old buildings linked by station canopies rescued from the old Furness Railway Millom and Bransty stations. The atmosphere, enhanced by hanging baskets and FR squirrel seats, was

highly commended in the 1983 and 1984 Best Restored Stations competition. Only 'Skid Row', an accommodation coach beloved of Ratty's volunteers, remains as a somewhat historic blot on the landscape! Along the tracks are associated facilities that include a restored watermill, the 'Ratty Arms' public house and tracts of farmland and forest.

New workshop facilities at Ravenglass have enabled virtually all work on locomotives to be done on site. In 1976, the shops completed *Northern Rock*, a powerful narrow gauge style locomotive combining the best features of all the other engines. In 1978 the Belle Vue Class 30 was saved and restored first cosmetically, then mechanically with the help of British Nuclear Fuels apprentices. As *Synolda* it forms the centrepiece of the new museum, and far from Sand Hutton, is a joy to hear crackling up the valley on a special outing. The most recent addition to the steam fleet is the 0-4-2T *Bonnie Dundee* from the gasworks of that city. It was converted from 2ft gauge before entering service in 1982. The existing locomotives receive regular shopping each winter and are now fitted with airbrake equipment. *River Irt* was earlier restored to a narrow gauge appearance and

Staff, preservation society members in period costume and railway dog pose in front of *Northern Rock* on its day of commissioning into traffic at Ravenglass, 29 May 1976. (*Nick Stanbra*)

received a new boiler in 1978. Another new boiler fitted to *River Esk* in 1983 took the railway to the forefront of steam development, as modifications allow gas producer combustion, the object being complete combustion of all varieties of coal.

Diesels operate at Ravenglass for early, extra or works trains. In 1969, the line received *Shelagh of Eskdale* completed by Severn Lamb to support two of the Muir Hill quarry tractors. In 1977, *Royal Anchor* was replaced by the *Silver Jubilee* railcar set for use on light trains. In 1980 the workshops produced *Lady Wakefield*, a completely new B-B, to a design closely followed by the RH&DR No 12. The original Muir Hill is now a restored museum piece, but its partner was rebuilt and rebodied in 1984 to face another 50 years use. 'Station pilot' is a Greenbat 0-4-0 battery locomotive rescued from a fireclay mine near Sheffield.

Coaching stock has seen tremendous changes, with the steady acquisition of closed and semi opens, developed from the 1967 prototypes. Large windows are essential. Some coaches have heating for winter service and others wheelchair access: these were commissioned by the late Sir Douglas Bader in 1982. However, the traditional open coaches are still most popular in fine weather and new ones were built in 1985 to a 1969 pattern.

In 1976 the line entered the high-tech era with its use of radio for centralised train control from the Ravenglass signal box. Though unique on preserved lines, the system heralded the micro processor based system now used by British Rail on rural lines. In spite of such willingness to abandon convention to gain efficiency, the R&ER keeps its traditional friendliness and customs such as locomotive gatherings. The 1976 Passenger Centenary and 1981 Twenty-First anniversary of Preservation saw memorable gatherings of visitors, while 1985 saw the return of *Green Goddess* to celebrate 60 years of the Paxman connection. These years of development are the direct result of the support of Lord Wakefield of Kendal, chairman from 1968 to his death in 1983, and future security was assured when his family pledged to keep the line running 'as if he were here'.

Less secure has been the Fairbourne Railway which faced upheaval after 1985. It had survived the storm damage of 1977 which required replacement of ¾ mile of track near the Ferry.

In 1980 track and stock were nearly transferred to the Medina Valley in the Isle of Wight. Finally after much uncertainty the line was taken over in 1984 by the Ellerton family, who had operated the spectacular but shortlived 12¼in gauge Reseau Guerledan in Brittany in 1978-9. Changes began at Fairbourne as *Ernest W Twining* left for storage with the Sutton Park stock, while *Rachel* and some coaches went to Wigan followed by *Katie* now renamed *Shôn*. *Sîan* was rebuilt as an American outline Sandy River style locomotive and renamed *Sydney*, and parts of *Sylvia* were rebuilt in the General Motors outline diesel *Lilian Walter*. In 1985 these hauled a set of the 12¼in coaches running on temporary 15in gauge bogies; this 'Seatrain' connected with a railway owned ferryboat.

Fairbourne Station was renamed Gorsaf Newydd, radically altered by the new platform on a concrete raft that now covered the stream. New locomotive sheds and nine road carriage shed were linked by multi-gauge track to the old building, now a workshop. The other stations have Welsh names too, Golf House now being rendered in a fairly extensive translation as Gorsafawddacha'idraigddanheddogladdo-lonpenrhynareurdraethceredigion. More entertainment comes when children are invited to 'wind up' the locomotive by the large key carried by the guard! The last scheduled passenger train on the 15in gauge was on 15 September 1985, after which work began to regauge from the Porth Penryn end. Four half-scale narrow gauge locomotives will handle services in future. After 70 years the only memories of the old ways will be *Count Louis* on a token length of 15in gauge track in a museum.

Other small lines have experienced differing fortunes. Alexandra Palace closed in 1970 and its stock went to Knowsley Safari Park near Liverpool. The Porthcawl line survives virtually unchanged. At Southport the Lakeside Railway changed hands in 1969 and lost its steam locomotives. The Barlow diesels *Duke of Edinburgh*, *Prince Charles* and *Golden Jubilee 1911-61* were joined in 1971 by the Severn-Lamb *Princess Anne*, a scale 'Western' type. However in March 1983 the Greenly/Bassett-Lowke Class 10 *George the Fifth*, and Class 20 *Princess Elizabeth* returned for a steam weekend with Class 30 *Synolda*. The success of this prompted the acquisition of *Red Dragon*, formerly *Prince Edward of Wales* from Margate,

A fine contrast in large Atlantics is provided by this 1976 picture of the line at Belle Vue. The nomadic Barnes engine *Railway Queen* is to the left while *Prince Charles* (formerly *Synolda*) makes ready to draw coaches out from the carriage shed/tunnel. (*D. Holroyd*)

which is being restored with new frames in the railway's workshops.

At Rhyl events have been traumatic with the closure of the line in 1969 after a dispute about the site lease. Tracks were lifted in 1970 and locomotives dispersed – *Joan* to Belle Vue, *John* to Alton Towers, and *Billy* to Rhyl Council as a reminder of better times. After the closure of Belle Vue in 1977, *Joan* ran briefly at Steam-town. Back at Rhyl, the track was relaid mainly along the old route by Alan Keefe Ltd in 1978, and his concession taken over by Leslie Hughes in 1980. *Clara* from Dudley Zoo, *Michael* and *Billy* were used, while Hughes obtained the stock from Margate and the other homeless Barnes locomotives. *Michael* went to Dudley in 1981 and was followed by the 'Margate 104', returning by October 1984. Four Barnes' locomotives were again on the strength at Rhyl. All trains operated with steam for the simple reason that the ex-Margate I/C locomotive could barely pull two coaches while the newly overhauled *Louise* (ex-*Railway Queen*) could manage seven.

Yet again, though, in 1985 there were fears for the future at Rhyl since the local council had announced that the line would not reopen in 1986.

The line at Dudley continues an erratic existence, losing the Guest diesels when the site closed in 1979, being extended to run briefly with steam, and in 1984 with the Rapidorail electric railcar built the previous year for Flamingoland in Yorkshire. Simple by comparison has been the story of the 15in gauge line at Bressingham, which started from an almost impromptu trip by Alan Bloom to Cologne to see the three Krupp Pacifics in store. Since construction in 1937, these locomotives had only run at the original Dusseldorf exhibition, a 1950 line in the Rheinpark in Cologne, the 1953 Munich Transport Exhibition and a line in the Bundesgartenschau at Cologne in 1958, latterly being stored. Nos 1662 *Rosenkavalier* and 1663 *Männertrau* and 20 coaches by Hardingen of Dusseldorf arrived in England in December 1972 to run in the following season. By 1974 a 2¼ mile circuit was completed and now makes two interesting flat crossings with the 2ft gauge Nursery line to form the Waveney Valley Railway. *Rosenkavalier* has made visits to both the R&ER in 1976 and the RH&DR in 1980 there meeting the third of the trio No 1664, *Black Prince*. In 1981 Bill Stewart's *Flying*

'British-US Zone' is displayed on the standard gauge wagons. The Krupp Pacific *Rumpelstilzchen* is seen at Munich in 1953. (*Bressingham Steam Museum*)

The Whorlton Lido Railway. In June 1976 Class 20 Atlantic *King George*, still bearing the legend 'Lakeside Miniature Railway' on its tender hauls a train past the quarter scale *Flying Scotsman* built by Bill Stewart. (*D. Holroyd*)

Scotsman joined the Waveney Valley fleet.

New lines have continued to be laid to 15in gauge as operators recognise the commercial advantages of seating passengers two aside, and the chances to use stock from redundant lines. Another significant influence has been a David Curwen design, built and promoted by Severn Lamb Ltd of Stratford. The 2-8-0 Rio Grande steam outline petrol/diesel/LPG powered locomotive is the workhorse of many amusement parks, giving reliable service at sites like Blackpool Zoo since 1972, Tramore, Galway, in Eire since 1973, Craigtoun near St Andrews from 1976, and as far afield as Belgium, the United States and the United Arab Emirates. Most lines are simple single track or loops. However, one of the most attractive sites in the dunes around Fleetwood's Marine Lake was not proof against vandals, lasting only from 1975 to 1982.

At Whorlton Lido, the Minimum Gauge was chosen when Raymond Dunn was able to secure *King George*, the former Southport Class 20 in 1971. However his desire to extend along the River Tees near Barnard Castle was thwarted by planning restrictions, so the line remains half a mile long with two balloon loops. It hosted Bill

Stewart's *Flying Scotsman* from 1976 to 1980 but was usually worked by *Wendy*, a Colby-Simkins diesel. In 1983 a Rio Grande steam outline diesel was obtained from Lambton Pleasure Park where it had run since 1976. In 1985 Albion Class *John* joined them from static display at Alton Towers.

The other Class 20 from Southport, *Princess Elizabeth*, had a nomadic life in Bill McAlpine's collection before finding a home at Steamtown, the LMS depot at Carnforth, Lancs. Here the management realised the value of the economic operation of 15in compared with standard gauge. In 1978, 1000yd of track were opened from the Keer site entrance, through the old engine shed and a passing loop at Central, out into the wilds of Crag Bank. Both ends connect with the standard gauge operating line. There was once a serious proposal to extend to Morecambe. German coaches contemporary with the 1937 Krupp locomotives and some by Guest, rejoice in names like *Marks and Spencer*, and *Laurel and Hardy*. The rebuilt Class 10 *George the Fifth* joined the fleet after its stay at Longleat. A mainstay is the diesel *Royal Anchor*, formerly at Ravenglass. Other diesels including Guest *Tracy-Jo*, and Anderson *Dr Diesel* came from the Pleasurerail operation at Blenheim Palace opened in 1975. The Guest Pacific now at Steamtown as *Prince William*, ran there too as *Sir Winston Churchill* contrasting in size with the Heiden 0-4-0 *Tekkel*. Blenheim currently uses Guest Co-Bo *Anna* formerly at Dudley Zoo; its sister from Dudley now runs on a ¾ mile long line at Cricket St Thomas Wildlife Park, Somerset, having previously been at Weymouth.

After operating for some years at Severn Beach, Leslie Anderson took his diesels and the overhead electric railcar *Amber Arrow* to a new site at Longleat House in Wiltshire. Running began in 1965 from a terminus close to the house to a large balloon loop alongside the lake. By 1968 a steeply graded branch line was extended to a terminus high above. Steam was introduced in 1967 with the Curwen designed Berwyn Engineering 0-6-0 *Muffin* with its narrow gauge outline. Another Curwen design, built this time by Severn Lamb in 1970, was the 0-6-2T *Dougal* which was followed by a Bo-Bo diesel-hydraulic railcar now called *Lenka*. Anderson moved some stock away in 1974 in preparation for what in the event proved to be the abortive Axe & Lyme Valley Light Railway scheme, though later sold

Not all the attractions at Steamtown, Carnforth are standard gauge and main line machines! Here Class 10 Atlantic, *George the Fifth*, formerly at Longleat, poses at Keer Station. (*Steamtown, Carnforth*)

Dougal back to the current Longleat operator. Under the management of John Hayton the Longleat track has been completely renewed from the ballast up, though without the branch. The extended main station has full signalling with interlocking in a smart signalbox. Alongside is a splendid Victorian style three road locomotive shed with workshop facilities, in which a new railcar was built in 1984.

Another Severn Lamb 0-6-2T *Zebedee* ran on the Lappa Valley Railway from its opening in 1974. This is built on 1¼ miles of the trackbed of the former Newquay to Chacewater line in Cornwall, from Benny Halt to a return loop at East Wheal Rose, a pleasure area around an old lead mine site. When the line was laid, steel rail was in short supply and aluminium was used instead. Daily operations involve 13 trips of 2½ miles shared with additional stock obtained from the Axe & Lyme Valley scheme, 0-6-0 *Muffin*, diesel 0-4-0 *Pooh*, and the now dieselised *Amber Arrow* renamed *Lappa Lady*.

Powys is a third Severn Lamb 0-6-2T built in 1974 for the then private Rhiw Valley Light Railway. By the time of its public opening in 1983, this extended 1½ miles. Further Severn Lamb equipment works a line at Blaise Castle regauged from 10¼in to 15in in 1978. This 600yd line uses battery powered conversions of former Axe & Lyme Light Railway coaches, and 0-4-2 *Foxglove*. Another Bristol line was at Cross Elms whose 0-4-0 petrol locomotive now runs at Pixieland near Bude. Such operations

MINIMUM GAUGE ON THE MAP – 1984.

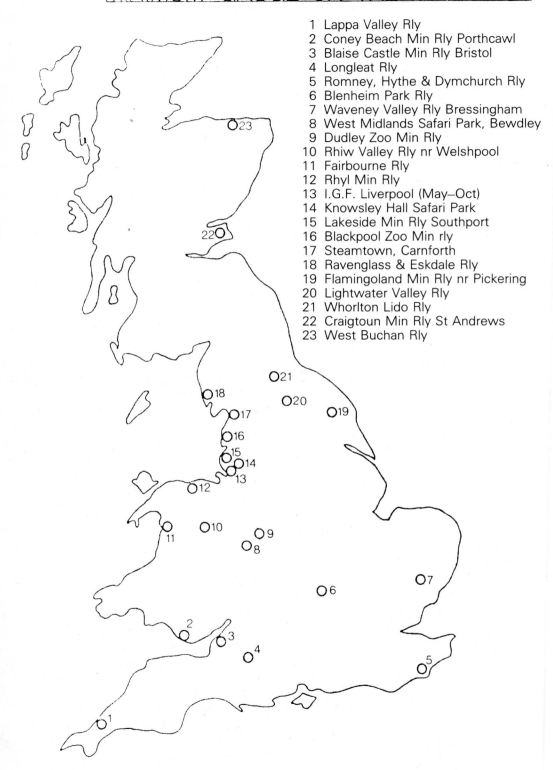

1 Lappa Valley Rly
2 Coney Beach Min Rly Porthcawl
3 Blaise Castle Min Rly Bristol
4 Longleat Rly
5 Romney, Hythe & Dymchurch Rly
6 Blenheim Park Rly
7 Waveney Valley Rly Bressingham
8 West Midlands Safari Park, Bewdley
9 Dudley Zoo Min Rly
10 Rhiw Valley Rly nr Welshpool
11 Fairbourne Rly
12 Rhyl Min Rly
13 I.G.F. Liverpool (May–Oct)
14 Knowsley Hall Safari Park
15 Lakeside Min Rly Southport
16 Blackpool Zoo Min rly
17 Steamtown, Carnforth
18 Ravenglass & Eskdale Rly
19 Flamingoland Min Rly nr Pickering
20 Lightwater Valley Rly
21 Whorlton Lido Rly
22 Craigtoun Min Rly St Andrews
23 West Buchan Rly

tend to be very ephemeral like the movements of four petrol locomotives built at Woolhope in Herefordshire for use on portable tracks. The 15in gauge private line tradition continues with the diesel-worked Woodland Railway in Surrey, a half mile track opened in 1982, the tracks around Arthington gasworks near Leeds, and a 70yd line at Ian Fraser's home at Arbroath. Here *Flower of the Forest* a 2-2-0 vertical boilered steam tram built at Ravenglass in 1985 lives in a shed erected by consent of the House of Lords. Still awaiting a line to run on, is the vertical boilered *Blue Pacific*. Built in Manchester in the 1930s it resides in Stockport after a brief holiday at Ravenglass.

Another new line was opened in Yorkshire in 1979 with a standard Severn Lamb Rio Grande 2-8-0. The Lightwater Valley Railway, near Ripon, is located in a theme park and has a ¾ mile circuit around a small artificial lake. When further stock was required, the opportunity was taken to acquire some more unusual stock from the North Eastern Railway operated by Tom Tate from 1971–6 near Durham. Mr Tate had acquired in 1964 the original *Little Giant* masquerading as *Robin Hood* from a fairground at South Shields. The locomotive was restored, then renamed at Ravenglass the following year. He also collected other interesting locomotives from the North East, including the pioneer Bassett-Lowke petrol locomotive from Saltburn which was restored as *Blacolvesley*, the Carland *Royal Scot* from Seaburn, and a Shire 4-4-0

A 'Scot' in the snow. The refurbished Carland Royal Scot back in steam at Lightwater Valley in January 1985. (*Peter van Zeller*)

Yvette that had been started in 1942 for the Redlands Railroad. The NER ran some 800yd in the grounds of Haswell Lodge, used genuine NER signals, and was graced by some attractive scale goods stock including a working steam crane. Sadly the site in the middle of the Durham coalfield was subject to vandalism, and some of the stock was moved to the Medina Valley project in the Isle of Wight but never ran. From 1980 much of the stock was acquired by Lightwater Valley where restoration work was done by John Henderson firstly on *Little Giant* then on the Scot, which was returned from its former dieselised state to steaming condition with the aid of a new boiler by Bill Stewart. At Lightwater, the stock is housed in yet another Victorian style shed quite in keeping with the surrounding theme park.

1981 saw the centenary of the first public revelation of the work of Sir Arthur Heywood, and this was marked by a special exhibition at the National Railway Museum in York. Its success attracted much comment in the museum and Royal Patronage on the occasion of a visit by the Prince and Princess of Wales. The exhibition traced in photographs and artefacts, the story of the Minimum Gauge while the larger items on display pointed out the major developments. A magnificent 3½in gauge model of *Ella* was loaned by Gervase Markham, and full size Heywood equipment was represented by *River Irt* from the R&ER, a wagon, and the open coach and bogie brake van from Eaton Hall. *Little Giant* and *Blacolvesley* represented the early work of Greenly and Bassett-Lowke, the former engine meeting the small Eaton brake again for the first time since 1905. The final flowering of the main line era was seen in

Hurricane, the Romney, Hythe & Dymchurch Royal engine.

The major consequence of this seems to have been the resurrection of the miniature railway concept of the turn of the century. The International Garden Festival at Liverpool in 1984 required a railway to move people around the site in vast numbers. Initial proposals for a 2ft gauge line were quickly amended to 15in with the greater availability of rolling stock. From August 1983 a spectacular 2½ mile line was laid, sweeping round the site in a convoluted loop that gave a short section of double track, with a branch line from the main station at Festival Hall to the Herculaneum Dock entrance. This replaced the original layout of an out and home loop from a main terminus at Herculaneum which was modified as the main gardens were planned. Indeed the site imposed fearsome gradients and curves and *The Railway Magazine* commented 'the layout of the main circuit appears to have been designed by an architect rather than a railway engineer'.

For motive power, the line was to employ *Black Prince*, *The Bug* and *Samson* (in an unfamiliar red livery) from Romney. From Ravenglass *Shelagh of Eskdale* and the *Silver Jubilee* railcar set (in the new Executive livery of the sponsor British Rail) were hired, the latter to work the branch line. However, test running with the coaches – six borrowed from Romney, and 21 newly built semi-opens from the Steamtown workshops – revealed just what was involved in steaming over a very demanding road. At short notice *River Irt* was fitted with vacuum brake equipment and sent from Ravenglass to bolster the steam fleet. At the opening on 2 May 1984, *Samson* and *Shelagh of Eskdale* were used to convey HM The Queen around the site.

The line was fully track circuited with colour-light signals by GEC, with additional warning lights worked at the 12 manned level crossings. Travel was free but the layout suffered from the use of common platforms for loading and unloading. Passengers were expected to travel only from one station to the next, and huge queues built up, so popular was the facility. By 15 October 1,920,880 passengers had been carried, and strong consideration was given to moves to keep a large part of the track in situ. However, lifting took place within hours of the closing of the Festival, and the stock returned to home bases or store soon after.

The future of 15in gauge seems assured with several lines under construction or in the pipeline. In 1984, the West Buchan Railway opened its first phase of 1¼ miles from Banff Harbour

The Minimum Gauge Centenary Exhibition at the National Railway Museum, York, October 1981 to March 1982. In the background is *Hurricane*, to the right *River Irt* with two Heywood coaches while in the foreground *Little Giant* and the Eaton brake recreate the atmosphere of the 1905 trials. (*Copyright National Railway Museum*)

INTERNATIONAL GARDEN FESTIVAL - LIVERPOOL
MINIATURE RAILWAY (May - October 1984.)

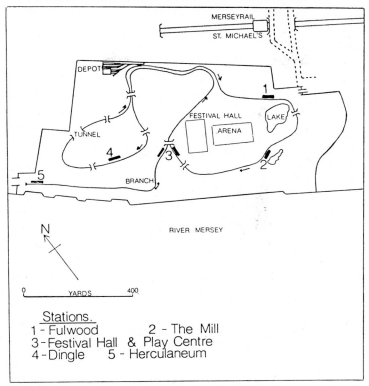

Stations.
1 - Fulwood   2 - The Mill
3 - Festival Hall & Play Centre
4 - Dingle   5 - Herculaneum

along the former British Railways trackbed to Tillynaught on 23 June. It has a Rio Grande 2-8-0 and coaches from Fleetwood, aided by the Dutch 0-4-0 *Chough* built by Heiden, and formerly at Romney, Blenheim and Bird Paradise at Hayle, Cornwall. It is hoped to rebuild the old overall station roof at Banff and extend to Whitehills to give a three mile run. The other locomotive from Hayle, Barlow's *Princess Anne* built for Butlins at Skegness, has joined *Rachel* from Fairbourne at Haighe Park in Wigan. In 1985 a steeply graded and convoluted loop of track was under construction to provide an interesting route for the latest acquisition, the 2-4-2 formerly *Katie* from the Fairbourne. Also under construction is a mile of 110 volt overhead electric tramway from the Conwy Valley Railway Museum at Bettws-y-Coed.

The popularity of the line at the Liverpool International Garden Festival has led to the inclusion of 15in gauge railways in plans for theme parks like that proposed for Lancaster's Williamson's Park and future Garden Festivals at Glasgow and Gateshead. The entire Liverpool

IGF railway from coaching stock to station buildings was taken to Britannia Park, a theme park being developed near Derby. The first half mile of a track intended to surround a lake, and branch out through the park, was opened in July 1985. The locomotive *Shelagh of Eskdale* was on loan from the R&ER for the first season of the new park which alas ended inauspiciously with the appointment of a receiver.

Thus the development of 15in gauge railways continues to be a complex, confusing, yet ever fascinating story. Lines and locomotives continue to give pleasure to a world that their original builders could not have conceived. Bassett-Lowke and Greenly would have been quite at home planning the International Garden Festival Railway. Yet Sir Arthur Heywood would have felt chagrin that his engineering principles were still cherished, while the opportunity to change rural England two generations before motor transport did was missed. For the future, those principles offer the railway operator the capacity to handle large volumes of passengers that smaller gauges cannot, with an economy envied by the larger gauges.

Driver Richard Batten looks somewhat apprehensive in the royal presence on the opening day of the International Garden Festival at Liverpool, 2 May 1984. The 'Royal Train' comprises the RHDR Director's Saloon hauled by the 4-8-2 *Samson*. (*Liverpool Daily Post and Echo*)

Festival Hall station of the Liverpool International Garden Festival line. All 'Ratty' motive power is in evidence as *River Irt* connects with the *Silver Jubilee* railcar working the Herculaneum branch. (*Peter van Zeller*)

CHAPTER TEN

PULLING POWER I
Development of Steam Locomotives

Many minimum gauge locomotives continue to operate. Their long lives are due to successful engineering to cope with widely different conditions from parks and private gardens to the seaside and the mountains. Great care has been given to their outward appearance to attract the passengers crucial to their survival. *Pearl* certainly has visual appeal as one of the largest model locomotives used for display, but it could also have given a performance of some speed given the right rail conditions for its 20in driving wheels. The profiles are sufficiently overscale to prove *Pearl* was designed to run even if records of this no longer exist.

Heywood made no concession to scale, build-

'Works grey'. *Muriel* at Duffield Bank in 1894. (*L&GRP/ David & Charles*)

ing his first locomotive *Effie* cheaply to experiment with the aim of perfecting the small locomotive. With launch type boiler in which the cylindrical firebox was fully contained, and inside Stephenson valve gear, it was little different from the Crewe Works 18in gauge locomotives. It ran 3,000 miles 'with none but trifling repairs' and from this was developed the classic Heywood engine with its many special features. *Ella* of 1881 was 'a locomotive suitable for military purposes, to afford great power on a narrow gauge and able to take sharp curves, at the same time avoiding the complication of the double bogie system'.

The wheels were on sleeves that could radiate to curves as sharp as 25ft radius, while the axles pegged inside the sleeves kept a fixed alignment in the locomotive frames. The centre wheels had

sideplay which caused the outer wheels to turn on ball joints, moved by a linkage. This necessitated outside frames and valve gear. Heywood devised a drive rod from the big end of the connecting rod to a straight expansion link above it out of the dirt, a modification of Brown's Swiss tram locomotive gear. From *Effie* came rubber block springing and big end brasses that twisted to cope with the track. The launch boiler by Abbott's of Newark again avoided the need for carrying wheels which would have reduced adhesive weight, as the locomotive balanced fore and aft with the driver on board. More sophisticated were the combined lever/screw reverser, blower opened by closing the regulator, and steam sanders. Most elegant was the deep green livery with brass dome set off to perfection by burnished rods, cranks and steam chest. Most remarkably, Heywood had largely built the locomotive himself from raw castings from his foundry. On test for the military, *Ella* took a load equal to its own weight up a 1 in 9 grade. But the design was quietly forgotten by the British Army in spite of successfully running 50 miles with maximum load at 18mph. The German Feldbahn however developed the Klein-Lindner system from Heywood's radiating gear.

In print, Heywood recommended 'four

The end of a line: *Katie* née *Shelagh* being dismembered at Balderton on 4 September 1942. The rear radial axle is particularly apparent. (*J. G. Vincent*)

wheeled simple locomotives are cheapest and best', although by 1894 he had applied the radial gear to the 0-8-0T *Muriel*, this time with two sliding wheelsets. Improvements over *Ella* included balanced cranks, enclosed crankpins and an adjustable blast nozzle to avoid lifting the thin fire when working hard. With 18in wheels and 6½in by 8in cylinders *Muriel* could haul eight bogie coaches with 120 passengers, as her chassis continues to do under *River Irt*. Less successful was his four-wheeled locomotive *Katie* of 1896 for the Eaton Railway. It ran well on test, but proved hard on the ash ballasted track and prone to violent slipping on greasy rails in the woods. The final development was the 0-6-0T *Shelagh*, little smaller than the 0-8-0T and capable of managing the work in all conditions so well that the design was exactly repeated in 1916 for *Ursula*. As built they had brief operating lives, though work at Eaton involved travelling 2000 miles a year. The substantial chassis construction was proven in use but daily work showed the weakness of the launch boiler with its limited heating surface of the dryback firebox and a third of its volume as ashpan. From the number of new 'furnaces' supplied by Abbott's for these boilers up to 1924, they seem to have suffered from low water damage and choking with solid deposits, tested beyond the limit by Eaton and Eskdale's severe grades.

In complete contrast the Cagney engines resembled a full size prototype, the American coal burning 4-4-0. There were 2in steel bar

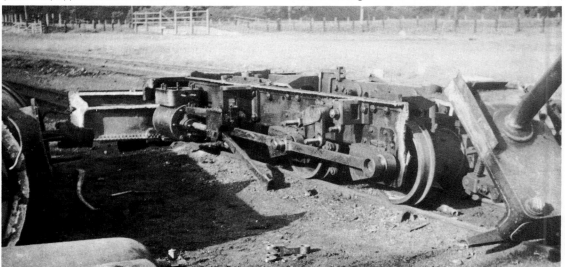

The Liverpool exhibition of 1913 boasted a 500yd minia-ture railway with a Herschell-Spillman 4-4-0 as motive power. The 'biggest mountain scenic railway ever con-structed' did somewhat dwarf the Minimum Gauge! (*Derek Brough*)

frames with massive smokebox saddle-cum-bogie stretcher. The boiler barrel continued to form the smokebox, while the firebox sat on the frames for the full width between the wheels. Castings for the cab sides concentrated adhesion weight on the driving wheels. Other detailed castings formed the smokebox front with the name of supplier and building date cast into the ring. Sophisticated fittings included rocking grate, and feedwater preheating coil in the smokebox, but there were no springs! They were lively runners with great acceleration given by the tiny 10in wheels and 3in diameter × 5in stroke cylinders – the same 2:1 ratio recom-mended by Heywood. The 12in gauge design could pull 5000lb but the 15in could pull double or 24 passengers in three bogie coaches. The Blakesley example could have handled coal trucks to the hall in 1903 and the same engine

(almost certainly) travelled round the Romney 66 years later. George Barlow drove five miles in 31min with it steaming against the injector 'in a very game fashion'.

Similar engines by Herschell-Spillman Co had a true wagon top firebox and slightly larger cylinders and wheels. They were robust enough for one to run daily along a 500yd track at Liverpool for 4½ months, and another to survive at Southend from 1907 to 1938. With their exposed pipework and un-English features, the Americans offended Greenly and Bassett-Lowke at the 1901 Glasgow Exhibition. Their importation, though, revealed a potential market for a British product.

Greenly had by 1904 outlined an 0–4–2T with launch boiler, 12in driving wheels and 3½ × 5in cylinders for estate work – possibly for Blakesley. Bassett-Lowke wanted to build 'the largest working model railway locomotive' so *Little Giant* was designed as a 4-4-2 express machine. Main frames were ¼in plate with bar stretchers as in model practice. The 18in driving wheels were set close together to go round sharp curves. The trailing axle had inside bearings and limited the firebox within the frames. Otherwise the boiler was much bigger than a Cagney and ample for the 3¼ × 5in cylinders. The trials at Eaton on Greenly's birthday proved this when *Little Giant* moved 13½ tons including *Shelagh*. It averaged 17¼mph with 5 tons up to the Hall, and returned with 2½ tons at a spirited 26.4mph. Greenly thought it was too fast and that bigger cylinders would increase its capacity. Later at Blackpool, it pulled four bogie coaches with 48 passengers, roaring up the 1 in 80 throwing sparks into ladies' hats. On busy days, there were 120 trips around the quarter mile circuit with fuel costs of ½d a mile. However the site in the dunes 'considerably increased working expenses and wear and tear'.

Demand was slow for the three sets of frames cut out with *Little Giant*'s but improvements were made from No 12 *Entente Cordiale*. Bogie tenders, and boilers with fewer but larger tubes helped the engines to run over 100 miles a day, loaded to the limit, with minimal standing time. The narrow firebox was not easy to fire, and with longer runs in view, Greenly designed an Atlantic and Pacific for Narrow Gauge Railways Ltd. As they were being built, Bassett-Lowke was also completing No 21 *Prince of Wales* for Llewelyn with enlarged boiler, bored out cylinders and other *Little Giant* castings.

At 2¼ tons for the Atlantic and three tons for the Pacific, the NGR designs had enough adhesion to pull 70 and 100 passengers. They had bigger wheels, and cylinders with valves on top, like the Cagneys, worked by inside Stephenson gear. The rear axle had outside bearings like the Class 20, now allowing a wider

The increasing stature of the Bassett-Lowke Atlantics. From left to right, Class 20 *Princess Elizabeth*, Class 10 *George the Fifth* and Class 30 *Synolda*. This family portrait taken at Southport in March 1983. (*Neville Fields*)

Wootten firebox to be fitted which had a basket grate to carry a deep fire – to reduce spark throwing and damage to hats! Cecil J. Allen tested *Synolda*, the first Class 30 Atlantic, at Sand Hutton, averaging 13mph with eight tons, and reaching 30mph with two coaches. He wrote '. . . Travelling tender first at a (scale) speed equivalent to 120mph – prevented a stop watch reading'!

This prompted Jack Howey to commission the Class 60 Pacific from Bassett-Lowke and to prove it to be the fastest 15in gauge locomotive. In July 1914, Allen recorded the performance of *John Anthony* at Eaton. It started a 16¾ ton load and averaged 13.8mph blowing off throughout. They held back from driving 'at her full capacity downhill or fully 40mph would have been realised'. Playing trains at this level was a supreme indulgence; in contrast the newly reopened Eskdale Railway aimed to serve its community. Running trains to a timetable throughout the year forced a major development of 15in gauge locomotive designs.

Greenly commented as operation began 'while the engines at Eskdale are doing excellent work on . . . a rather rough track with heavy grades . . . such engines will not on a five year basis, show themselves an economic investment'. He suggested narrow gauge models could offer greater power, showing an 0-6-0 goods engine with 5 × 8in cylinders, 16½in driving wheels and 5sq ft of grate. He proposed to use totally enclosed motion which could be removed for maintenance, and that the driver should sit inside the tender below cab roof height. Greater firebox capacity and complete driver protection could be given by articulation like a single Fairlie. A later 2-8-4T was drawn up at Jubb's of Sheffield probably for the Sand Hutton extensions. More practical was Greenly's May 1918 'Estate locomotive with the highest possible tractive effort at

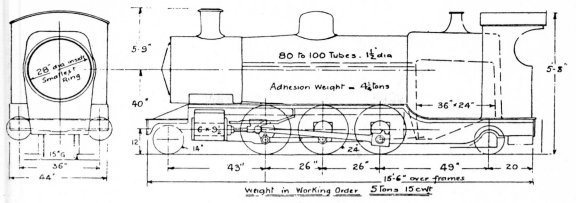

A sketch design for a heavy 15in gauge goods locomotive by Henry Greenly in 1918.

speeds up to 18mph'. This narrow gauge 2-6-2 would pull 20 tons up 1 in 100 with 6 × 9½in cylinders, 24in driving wheels and 5sq ft grate. Though influenced by John Coit's one-third scale 18in gauge American engines, it was so close to the design evolved for *Northern Rock* at Ravenglass a lifetime later that one can only admire his foresight. But without sponsors the designs remained on the drawing board.

Commercial operators still wanted miniature outlines, and Greenly designed the Albion class 4-4-2 for construction at the Albion Works of Albert Barnes at Rhyl. Virtually a Class 30 boiler sat on a simplified chassis. Inside rear truck bearings allowed the locomotive to negotiate 80ft radius S bends. There were bigger cylinders, stronger motion and such visual differences as continuous splashers and six-wheel tender compared with the earlier design. The first *Joan* was completed in August 1920 and 'simply romps away with 80 passengers' reported the designer with delight. Anticipating a buoyant market for such machines, six were started though it was another decade before all were completed. Barnes himself recalled that each locomotive took a year to 18 months to finish.

At Ravenglass meanwhile, experience was hard earned; luckily passengers enjoyed pushing trains up hills! The scale model locomotives were a great attraction, easy to drive and steamed economically. The Heywoods burned four times the coal as they did coke, had no shelter, and had to be driven by the regulars rather than the summer students. Whitsun weekend 1920 found all the model locomotives under repair and *Ella* took all trains including one of 265 people! In 1921 the new Pacific *Sir Aubrey Brocklebank* hauled 10 tons for the return

trip in 90min to impress Greenly. He had suggested a continuation of the Heywood type but later wrote 'the goods engines of Sir Arthur Heywood which I had placed so much hope before I saw them at work at Eskdale, are not provided with ordinary locomotive boilers and cannot compare in full efficiency with the model engines. I have just piloted with *Sans Pareil* a train of 120 people over the seven miles of 1 in 40 on about 60lb of coke'. Experiments with oil firing took place on this engine – passengers avoided bombardment with cinders but had to endure fumes instead!

Granite traffic from Beckfoot quickly revealed the weaknesses of the existing types, and prompted the design of a prototype for the R&ER conditions. A proposed scale model 2-8-2 was rejected in favour of a design evolved from first principles. Greenly and Mitchell decided *River Esk* should 'first do the mineral traffic required of it; secondly more or less completely protect the engineman in rough weather; and thirdly deal with a passenger train of open coaches in as clean and easy a manner as possible at the average timetable speeds, and to present to the eye of the observer a pleasing outline of a scale model character'. First 180lb boiler pressure, 5¼ × 8½in cylinders and 17½in driving wheels would give double the tractive effort of the largest Pacific. Secondly the driver would sit in the tender below the extending cab roof, after tests with a linoleum mock up proved visibility would be adequate. Thirdly 4.7sq ft of grate and a large firebox would make it steam easily with low smokebox vacuum. Finally cab and boiler mountings would be to one-third scale with a Great Western flavour to please Sir Aubrey Brocklebank although this 'makes not the slightest difference to its efficiency as a loco-motive'.

Personal contacts led to an order for a 2-8-2 mineral locomotive going to Davey, Paxman in May 1923. This firm built boilers and Lentz poppet valve engines for refrigeration plants, and offered to fit Lentz cylinders instead of slide valves and Greenly gear. Paxman Patent valve gear designed by Chief Draughtsman Charles Barnes had a Hackworth slide within an eccentric cage on the second driving axle. R&ER Engineer Cauchi introduced the Krauss pony truck guiding the leading driving wheels. Greenly managed to insist on ¾in thick frames for maximum adhesive weight, but failed in other features as he was only put in charge of building half way through the contract. The locomotive was bench tested in October and delivered on 18 December 1923. Urgently needed, it was tested in the snow to reveal

(top)
Romney, Hythe and Dymchurch Railway 4-8-2 *Man of Kent* stands completed at Davey, Paxman Ltd. Capt. Howey did not like the straight nameplates and the locomotive ran nameless through the 1927 season before being finally named *Hercules*. (*Richard Bailey*)

(below)
Krauss Pacific *Springerie* at Stuttgart in 1976. This powerful looking locomotive was built in 1950 but to the original 1925 design of Roland Martens. (*R. A. Bowen*)

problems starting loads on hills, because of restricted cut-off or sticking valves. By April Greenly had returned twice to Colchester with the eccentric cage shattered in a violent slip. 'When speed falls on a bank . . . the driver may open up on one of the weak beats, the following good stroke giving an impulse which starts the slipping'. There was 'original sin in the design'!

In June 1924 Greenly drafted specifications for 'Pacific type Locomotives 15in gauge for Count Zborowski of Higham and J. E. P. Howey of Sunningdales' following their visit to see *River Esk* in action. A boiler like *Esk* could feed two 5¼ × 8½in cylinders, but this time with piston valves, Clupet rings and Walschaerts valve gear. Light high grade steel motion and carefully balanced 25½in driving wheels would avoid the *Esk*'s rough ride and allow speeds of 40mph. Again a one-third scale outline was proposed, this time following closely the Gresley Great Northern Pacifics of which *Flying Scotsman* was the centre of a display at the then current Wembley Exhibition. Whatever his intentions, Zborowski ordered two Pacifics from Davey, Paxman, with Greenly to supervise work. The order was placed in July, though the date was later erased, and work halted after Zborowski's death. Howey continued construction and took the first Pacific *Green Goddess* for trials at Ravenglass in June 1925. These were very satisfactory as the locomotive managed a 34 ton load in comparison to the *Esk*'s 29 tons. With 20 coaches, average speeds of 22½mph were possible. '35mph was obtained with ease but the character of the Eskdale line would not allow the hoped-for speed of 40mph'. At full speed 'the engine appeared to go to sleep'. Further trials were made to compare the simple vacuum brake and the Westinghouse fitted to the locomotive, with the expectation of public running somewhere in the future.

Greenly also helped at this period with advice for Roland Martens in the design of the Krauss one-third scale Pacifics for the 1925 Munich Transport Exhibition. Martens still had the ½in scale coal fired model locomotives designed by Greenly in 1913, and consulted him throughout construction. To cope with a 1 in 50 bank, they had 500mm (19⅝in) driving wheels and 150 × 200mm (nearly 6 × 8in) cylinders with piston valves and Walschaerts valve gear. The boiler had increased grate area and a copper firebox to 'allow for the inferior quality of German fuel'.

Adhesion was enhanced by the weight of the 20mm thick bar frames, which had adjustable wedges in the horns, laminated springs all round and side lever control of the front bogie. They could start a full 10 coach train on the bank, developed 35 indicated horse power and steamed perfectly even after six hours continuous hard work. Martens thanked the R&ER for its help 'I wish I could see them on your Eskdale line', a wish never fulfilled in spite of the numbers of the K3/6 Pacifics. Martens was in a strong position to offer to build engines for the Romney, Hythe & Dymchurch scheme but only a modified 0-4-0 of the Krauss standard 600mm gauge type was delivered. *The Bug* cost £350, one-third of the Paxman engines, was delivered in three months and was ideal for construction trains over unconsolidated tracks.

The application for the RH&DR Light Railway Order was posted with another order for a Pacific from Davey, Paxman. Four more engines were ordered when the LRO was granted, using common patterns and boiler parts, but adapted to the needs of the new line. Two 4-8-2s had 19½in driving wheels to move mineral traffic from a ballast pit near Hythe, though they proved equal in speed and more sure footed on heavy trains than the Pacifics. However there were problems in negotiating the small radius pointwork laid before these loco-

motives were ordered, that even running temporarily as 4-8-0s did not solve. When mineral traffic did not materialise, they spent long periods out of use. The other two engines were three cylinder Pacifics with independent Greenly radial valve gear on the inside rather than Gresley's conjugated valve gear of the full size engines, but otherwise as the early Pacifics. Greenly intended to have one as a Smith compound with a central high-pressure cylinder feeding outside low-pressure cylinders, but Howey did not want an uneven beat 'so we put up an intermediate water column to get the three-cylinder men through to their destination'. Terence Holder recalled 'unless everything was in perfect order they were most difficult engines to drive'. On a good rail they could use the extra 50% power; *Typhoon* once hauled 327 people, but adhesion restricted performance of all the Pacifics. High speed running soon revealed shortcomings: coil springs could not cope with the Romney track and were replaced by leaf springs where possible, smokebox steam driers were removed, and by 1937 both three cylinder locomotives were converted to two after problems with the inside valve gear.

Greenly's ultimate aim was to have two locomotives to his typical American outline used from 2½ to 12in gauges, this time to give drivers more shelter in winter. Davey Paxman castings from a cancelled order came to New Romney for assembly with Krauss K3/6 boilers, built with a batch of locomotives for Spain. However Greenly left the RHDR and his detail drawings

Doctor Syn, ex works, poses on Dymchurch turntable in April 1931. (*Rick Eyles Collection, courtesy National Railway Museum*)

'Can you build this?' Twining's sketch of the 2-4-2 for Dudley Zoo. The locomotive was eventually built in 1954 as *Katie*. (*Courtesy Raymond Dunn*)

went to the Yorkshire Engine Co where the Canadian Pacific 4-6-2s were assembled. In spite of fine details like the cast bufferbeams with pushpole sockets, smokebox doors and Vanderbilt tenders, they were apparently not good performers when new. Replaced valve gear parts still lay at New Romney after the war. Some parts also survived from the one-third scale Princess Royal Pacific, retrieved after the death of the builder H. C. S. Bullock in 1937. The frameplates were cut for the temporary bufferbeams fitted to *Shelagh of Eskdale* in 1981. Other designs proposed for the RHDR included a 2-8-2, 4-8-4s and after the war an amazing Duplex drive 4-4-4-4.

1937 also saw the final development of Martens' Pacifics built by Krupp for the Rhenische Bahn at the Dusseldorf exhibition. Cylinders 6½ × 10in give the highest tractive effort of all 15in gauge machines although the small grate area has to be forced to steam freely. After long periods in store, two run at Bressingham and the third had been at Romney, Ravenglass, Liverpool and even Japan!

Meanwhile at Ravenglass, a change of management stopped further 2-8-2s following *River Esk*. Ted Wright, the new engineer, thought the existing engines could be improved cheaply. *Muriel* again needed boiler work so the frames were extended to take a conventional boiler, while a tender was built for fuel and driver. As *River Irt*, the narrow gauge chassis looked odd with miniature cab etc, but it could pull. To quote Tom Jones' diary 'flower picking days were over'! More ambitious was the 4-6-6-4

River Mite using both scale Pacific chassis under a massive new boiler with cab and tender in a Modified Fairlie unit. It could pull 32 tons at 38mph, but the running gear wore under the strain and was sold to Barlow at Southport in 1940. Finally *River Esk* was converted to Walschaerts valve gear and larger piston valve cylinders, a move complicated by the alterations of the Yorkshire Engine Co to demonstrate their Poultney Patent Power Tender. Locomotive cut-off was limited to 50% and surplus steam was fed to an 0-8-0 unit under the tender. Instead of 29 tons, this four-cylinder machine could use the extra adhesive weight to pull 50 tons which C. J. Allen boasted 'the maximum tractive possibilities of so narrow a gauge'. In the event, the new Muir Hill tractors and the standard gauge line to Murthwaite took over the granite traffic completely. By 1933 the Poultney unit was isolated, after which the locomotive ran better without the inefficient rear cylinders!

Internal combustion took over on gauges larger than 15in, leaving steam building to the model engineers. Some of them built 15in gauge engines for private customers. Morse built American switcher 0-4-0 and 0-6-0 for the Dean's Mill line. George Barlow dissuaded Howey from buying them because of their scale wheel profiles. Trevor Guest found problems with his scale Stanier Class 5 4-6-0 to Twining's design, finished in 1946 for the regauged Dudley Zoo Railway. The firebox was too narrow and another similar locomotive was altered with a rear truck to carry a wide firebox before running at Fairbourne as 4-6-2 *Ernest W. Twining*. The 4-6-0 ran there too before its conversion to a Pacific named *Winston Churchill*. The Seaburn *Royal Scot* built by Carland in 1950 to a scaled up 10¼in gauge design had similar problems, resolved by replacing the boiler with a diesel engine. Restoration in 1984 incorporated a five element superheater in Bill Stewart's new boiler. Stewart had earlier completed to Greenly's designs, a quarter-scale LNER A3 *Flying Scotsman*, with full conjugated valve gear and three cylinders. Delightful to see and hear in action, it illustrates Greenly's versatility and wisdom in choosing overscale proportions for commercial running.

Such problems had filled the correspondence columns of the *Locomotive Magazine* in 1940 following publication of a sketch by Ernest Twining of a proposed 0-4-2 tender locomotive for passenger and light industrial use. A sketch from the same pen went to Trevor Guest with the request 'can you build this?' For the first time since Heywood, a 15in gauge locomotive was to look like a small locomotive in its own right rather than a model of the full size. By 1954, a 2-4-2 to be called *Katie* was under construction by Guest, with 5 × 8in cylinders, Twining valve gear and 20in driving wheels. With elegant tall chimney, dome and cab there was the classic British colonial flavour. Indeed tests were made to see if the Bagnall boiler would steam on coconut husks before its sale from Dudley Zoo for use on a West Indies plantation. A virtual repeat named *Sian* with sealed bearings to exclude sand was built for

Fairbourne in 1963. *Sian* was later to run on the R&ER with interesting results.

Two other designers with much experience in smaller gauges are Wilhelm van der Heiden and David Curwen. Heiden's Emett style 0-4-0s are 10¼in proportions enlarged to 15in track. Curwen's designs for Longleat are deceptively powerful, being capable of pulling 100 people on the level. Berwyn Engineering 0-6-0 tender locomotive *Muffin* of 1967, and Severn Lamb 0-6-2T *Dougal* have 12in driving wheels, 3½ × 5in cylinders with piston valves and Baker valve gear. Running boards of ½in plate make a strong structure with frames and bufferbeams, while axleboxes and other bearings have roller bearings. At Longleat traffic at peak times is too intense to allow regular steaming, but Lappa Valley sees both types in operation sharing the six month season of about 6,000 miles running. 1½cwt of coal give a day's service from lighting up to 30 miles with four coach trains. Interestingly the tender locomotive *Muffin* is preferred as it gives more space for the driver than the equally attractive narrow gauge tank, *Zebedee*.

Most lines have been well supplied with engines to cover their services and the need for maintenance. The R&ER however had to run *River Irt* and *River Esk* in continuous daily service each summer from 1952. The need to have additional steam locomotives to cover increasing traffic has led to the latest developments on 15in gauge rails. In 1957, Tom Jones proposed the marriage of the old *River Mite* boiler and the Poultney tender chassis. Then

Fairbourne elegance in 1966. The Twining sisters, *Sîan* and *Katie* at the passing loop. (*W. H. Foster*)

after the auction of the Ravenglass line, the R&ER Preservation Society funded the new *River Mite* from Clarkson's at York. The Poultney frames were extended with a rear cradle and Cartazzi radial boxes like the Romney engines, to carry an *Esk* boiler and 6 × 8½in cylinders. At first flexing frames caused leaking steampipes, inoperable sanders and wear from slipping. An extra frame stretcher has transformed *River Mite*'s reliability.

When it took to the road in 1967, traffic had grown to require all three steam locomotives in daily service from Whitsun to September. Brian Hollingsworth proposed a new standard locomotive using the *Esk* boiler and cylinders on an outside frame chassis with roller bearings. The narrow gauge appearance by changing cab and fittings could resemble a Rio Grande, a Russian or a British Colonial design. *River Amazon*, the latter, led to a visual alteration to *River Irt*, restoring a narrow gauge look when a new tender was needed in 1972. A boiler for the proposed new locomotive was ordered from Hunslet, after trials in November 1971 with a superheated machine from Romney. Experiments there with *Northern Chief* in 1954 had given 35% fuel saving from a two twin-element superheater, and all RHDR engines had subsequently received new boilers with this improvement. Appropriately *Northern Chief* caused a stir at Ravenglass with its general performance, although the benefits of superheating were held to be less than the costs of maintenance on a line with 40% coasting and burning coke instead of coal. The RH&DR made its own experiments to find a cleaner fuel than coal when *Winston Churchill* was converted to oil firing in 1973, shortly before oil price rises made this no longer viable financially.

Initially the new R&ER design was to be a 4-6-2T with slide valves; it was built as a 2-6-2 tender engine with 20in driving wheels and 6½ × 9in cylinders with piston valves to be capable of hauling 200 people. From 1973 raw plates and castings went into the railway's own workshops to emerge in March 1976 as *Northern Rock*. Detail design by Chief Engineer Ian Smith drew on the best features of existing locomotives including outside frames and centre sliding axle from Heywood, rear Cartazzi truck from Greenly. Unlike most machines it ran without teething troubles or major problems from its completion in time for the 1976 Centenary.

Celebrations concluded with a week of operation with engines from other railways. Veterans *Little Giant* and *Blacolvesley* were confined to Ravenglass station because of narrow wheel tyres. Scale models *Count Louis* and *Flying Scotsman* ran double headed as the Bassett-Lowke engines had in the early days. *Dr Syn* performed faultlessly, while *Rosenkavalier* struggled with its original draughting and steam drier but successfully worked the air brakes on its trains. In contrast *Sîan* from the Fairbourne surprised all by the efficient way it handled lighter trains. It was the answer for a potential white elephant given to the R&ER, a 2ft gauge Kerr Stuart Gasworks 0-4-0WT. It had been intended to regauge it to power a steam railcar, but a locomotive like *Sîan* would be more value. At *Sîan*'s visit in 1981, the conversion into an 0-4-2T using *Ella*'s side tanks was ready for steam trials. As *Bonnie Dundee*, it has cut the use of diesels in the peak season and works off-season six-coach trains. A recent costing exercise was done in response to outside enquiries for similar locomotives for new railways.

Thus there is a future for new steam locomotives, and with appropriate maintenance, all surviving machines could run indefinitely. *River Esk* for instance has just received its first completely new boiler since 1923, complete with over fire air tubes and exhaust steam fed into the ashpan on Porta's Gas Producer Combustion System. This enables almost any quality of coal to be burned without smoke or clinker, using a technique that will be at the heart of a new generation of full size steam locomotives if plans in the United States comes to fruition.

CHAPTER ELEVEN

PULLING POWER II
Development of Internal Combustion Locomotives

Petrolea at Blakesley was among the pioneer internal combustion locomotives of any gauge. Bartholomew, the designer, was a motoring enthusiast with a turntable in the garage to reverse the Humber. Alex Wyatt, his engineer built the 4-4-4 around the motor and three speed bi-directional gearbox with radiator at one end and a 6ft chimney at the other. It would haul six coal wagons up the 1 in 100 to the Hall or take the family down to the train 'at speeds of 30mph'. The benefits of instant power were clear and Bassett-Lowke and Greenly were thus able to propose 'an entirely new concept'. Externally it was a 4-4-4 tank version of *Little Giant* using common castings. Underneath a 12/14hp NAG car engine drove through a three-speed gearbox and separate reverse. The exhaust went up the chimney drawing air through the radiator hidden in the 'smokebox'; even the controls were like steam practice. Tested on delivery on 11 September 1909, it managed 5¼

Petrolea on estate duties at Blakesley circa 1906. The utilitarian appearance of the locomotive is obvious as are the splendid banner signals. The train is heading to the main line station past the loop around the park. (*Philip Kingston*)

tons on a 1 in 24 gradient and 32mph lightly loaded. From the flower show on, this new locomotive *Blacolvesley* virtually eclipsed steam on all duties.

In spite of its attraction, the design was not repeated, though Greenly proposed I/C locomotives for light railway schemes after the first world war. At this time the Eskdale line's daily service was wearing out the steam engines, with little return. By 1920 the Scooter had evolved, a light four-wheeled trolley with motor cycle engine. Fast with no reverse or brakes, they were manhandled to face the other way, and usually did not stop in time to avoid a nasty end! The 4hp *Douglas* could pull 12 people in the Sand Hutton saloon and a mail wagon. It was followed in 1923 by *Bunny*, the Crewe tractor conversion of a Ford T car adapted for the battlefield railways. It could pull five tons up a 1 in 20 at very low cost, but again had to be turned to go far backwards, this time on a built-in-jack. When it expired in summer 1925, within a month its components were part of a new locomotive.

This actually looked like a prototype with planked body on a bogie chassis like a District Railway electric. With Cecil J. Allen at the

The first of the hair-raising *Scooters* on the Ravenglass & Eskdale in 1921. The unlikely looking 'coach' conveyed the Royal Mail for Eskdale! (*Mary Fair*)

Dalegarth in July 1968. The stalwart Muir-Hill 'passenger tractor', on a relief train, displays a simple steam outline dating back to the 1930s. (*T. J. Edgington*)

throttle, it took the Eskdale line speed record with a down run of 15½min that stood 60 years later! After this Heywood's *Ella* almost had a two litre petrol engine and 150 amp electric drive, until a complete 38hp Lanchester car was mounted on the frames. I.C.L. No 2 could pull 38 tons, as much as the steam types. However Bert Thompson, its driver before and after, preferred the old *Ella*. In spite of extra ballasting, the rebuild was light on its feet.

The most successful locomotives at Ravenglass were the Muir-Hills with Fordson petrol/ paraffin engine, special gearbox and heavy cast frame. The 1927 original ran 20,000 miles in three years, and is still in running order with the original gearbox. One of the other two was modified in 1933 for passenger work with stabilising bogie and mock steam outline. After an incalculable mileage, it runs with great reliability with a Perkins diesel engine, and had a new industrial style body in 1984. Another standard industrial machine from Motorail of Bedford replaced the Eaton Railway steam locomotives in 1922. The Simplex 20hp bent-frame model gave good service until exchanged for a new straight frame locomotive in 1938. The latter survives in use at Romney.

After this experience it is strange that steam was used in the construction of the RH&DR and specified in the Light Railway Order. With winter trains no better patronised than the empty buses, a Ford T locomotive similar to the

The ubiquitous Severn-Lamb 'Rio Grande' 2-8-0, in this case caged at Blackpool Zoo. The splendid organ-pipe hooter is worthy of note. (*Blackpool Zoo Miniature Railway*)

R&ER machine was built by Theakston in 1928. Howey found it slow compared to his JAP scooter which did Romney to Hythe in 8½min for 8½ miles! This engendered a remarkable locomotive, the 1914 Rolls-Royce conversion that could pull four coaches at 60mph! With the approval of Rolls Royce it kept the bonnet and radiator through all its rebuilds, although it was more restrained with a Fordson engine, handling winter trains until its demise in 1961.

New construction elsewhere was internal combustion power often on larger than 15in gauge like Scarborough or Wicksteed Park. In the age of steam, mock steam outline was obligatory. In spite of their appearance the locomotives at Porthcawl have given over 50 years' service, *Coney Queen* initially using an infinitely variable hydraulic transmission derived from submarine controls. Another long-lived steam outline locomotive was the 2-4-0 built by Nigel Parkinson for Southend with the engine in the tender but the exhaust led to the chimney by a ratchet that gave four beats per wheel revolution! Parkinson had also built a bogie NER electric outline locomotive for Yarmouth using a 10hp Chapuis Dornier engine that could start a full load in top gear on the 1 in 72. More remarkable was the 1934 two-car set with Austin 7 engine and 6Kw generator that

could reach 12mph in its own length. In the power car the passenger accommodation had table service of lemonade and biscuits!

After 1945, war surplus provided suitable power units for Harry Barlow's LNER A4 outline 4-6-2s with a Fordson engine and Tilling Stevens generator in the tender powering another above the coupled wheels. Compared with steam, they did not need careful handling, unprofitable preparation time or regular wash-outs on Southport water. Seven more were built with slight variations and much name swopping, though sadly none of the Emett bodies survive.

Another prolific postwar builder was Trevor Guest whose diesels looked like the modern prototypes – a scale GW railcar as a locomotive for Dudley Zoo later supported by American and British styled locomotives, overscale to allow the driver to sit inside in comfort. His *Rachel* and *Sylvia* replaced earlier less sub-stantial machines at Fairbourne and have given over 20 years' service in the arduous conditions there. Scout car engines and transmissions give full speeds in both directions. Saddest of all locomotives is the half scale Vale of Rheidol 2-6-2 *Tracey-Jo* which has a complete steam chassis but has never managed to find a boiler to replace the Daimler engine. *Royal Anchor*, built by Lane in 1956, is a neat twin bogie design using naval gun mounting hydraulics for transmission. Romney trials proved it inefficient, but work at Ravenglass from 1961 proved the value of a modern diesel in support of the ageing Muir Hill tractors. Here the problem was stopping, for rough handling could burst hydraulic hoses which spread an oil slick on the track behind it. By 1968, finances allowed the 4-6-4 chassis built by Tom Jones to be completed by Severn Lamb to a design by David Curwen. *Shelagh of Eskdale* has a German twin cab outline, and a simple to operate drive in the Linde swashplate hydraulics. Initially continuous operation of heavy trains in hot weather caused problems, solved by upgrading the power train. Reliability was proved in its 19 months on the RHDR, and later the Liverpool International Garden Festival.

The same transmission is part of the classic Rio Grande steam outline 2-8-0 by Severn Lamb. It was designed by Curwen as a 10¼in gauge locomotive but built in 15in since 1971. The tender holds a Ford petrol or liquid petroleum gas engine and Linde pump with the hydraulic motor driving the locomotive rear axle. Stout bodywork and ⅞in frames give enough adhesion to haul 120 people on the level. Current specifications include an eagle on the headlight and 'electronic chuff' , but what counts with operators is the use of automotive parts which can be replaced from a garage.

Severn Lamb has also built diesel outlines from the 1971 Western *Princess Anne* for Southport to the magnificent one-third scale Belgian Class 205 for the Hengelhoef line. For

Les Anderson at Longleat the firm built *Lenka*, a single cab railcar with sanders and two pipe air brakes having six seats and power to pull six coaches. This unusual idea suits Longleat and an improved version is currently being built in the works there by John Hayton. A Deutz air-cooled engine also heats the 12-seat passenger compartment for off-season running.

The *Silver Jubilee* railcar developed at Ravenglass since 1976 started as a single coach. Now to cope with a useful level of traffic, two power cars can run with up to two trailers with controls linked by air and power cables. The unit was specially required for the branch line from the Herculaneum main entrance to the centre of the Liverpool International Garden Festival. Here with only 40 seats it carried approaching a third of the passengers on the whole line.

By 1975 great thought had been given to the design of a diesel for Romney, but finance could not be justified with spare steam locomotives available. The R&ER, however, faced inevitable problems with the 1927 Muir Hill, and began construction of a brand new diesel in 1979. To haul the heaviest trains of 10-12 coaches with ease, the power train was a Perkins 112hp diesel engine with an ex dump truck Twin Disc gearbox. With all wheels chain coupled and ballasted to four tons, it would have better adhesion than the other diesels. As a small gauge locomotive sees more shunting than the full size, one cab with all round vision was fitted. *Lady Wakefield* was completed in 1980 and quickly invited for trials at Romney. Here the 17 coach school train

Three generations of motive power at New Romney in May 1983. *Samson*, running wrong line, passes *Shelagh of Eskdale* and the new No 12 on shed. (*Peter van Zeller*)

Full signalling is evident in the station throat at Longleat as Severn-Lamb diesel *Lenka* approaches with a train on 18 September 1984. (*Peter van Zeller*)

needed two steam locomotives to be prepared right through the winter. Further ballasted to get under the Warren Bridge, *Lady Wakefield* performed as expected, hauling the whole train and a steam locomotive at 25mph. The design for TMA Engineering's diesel as RHDR No 12 was similar with shaft drive to all axles and detail improvements. Meanwhile, *Shelagh of Eskdale* was loaned to Romney for winters 1981–2, proving of value also in the summer operations with early and late trains, and as a stand by for busy periods, all without the two days lost each week washing out each steam locomotive. By the time of RHDR No 12's arrival *Shelagh of Eskdale* was working with a control trailer coach when propelling the empty stock. Subsequently its operation has proved the reliability of a single diesel.

Although this account has followed internal combustion power, some builders have chosen the simplicity of electric traction. Claud Lane's scale double-deck Darwen car had milk float motors taking 60 volts from an overhead wire. Garden fetes led to the short-lived Rhyl track which saw open single deck Blackpool Boat cars and a freelance open top double decker. Sold after the transfer to Eastbourne's 2ft gauge line, they still exist in private hands. More recently, milk float motors were used to power Blaise Castle's battery-powered railcars, and the Rapidorail International Metro train. Anderson had long held a belief that 15in gauge was suitable for low cost metro facilities that would fit into existing street patterns in the third world. Following early work at Severn Beach with *Amber Arrow*, plans exist for an eight-car articulated set. Half built, by 1984 the unit runs with a generator wagon for lack of a settled home at Flamingoland or Dudley has prevented erection of the special overhead catenary that energises in short sections.

CHAPTER TWELVE

CARS DE LUXE, TEAKS AND PULLMANS

Progress in Passenger Carrying

From Heywood to the present, one precept holds good: 'Man being an article of standard size . . .' You can scale down coaches and locomotives but you cannot scale down passengers. Thus two adults or three children can be seated side by side in 15in stock yet keeping within the limits of stability. To enhance the economic load that can be pulled the tare weight of the coach is usually less than the load it carries, but this creates problems for suspension and running gear.

Heywood's first coach was a basic four-wheel eight-seat open, the first of the garden railway tradition. But his next vehicles were remarkable in contrasting to full size stock and drew directly from Spooner's Festiniog bogie coaches. This concept enabled the floor of the 1881 16-seat saloon to be just inches above the rails, ensuring stability and headroom for a tall man to sit in tall hat and thus observe the proprieties! The bogies were hidden between the frames under the balcony seats. At first wooden frames were used with iron cast running gear and rubber block springs. To negotiate corners, couplings were attached to the bogies and one wheel on each axle was not fixed to it allowing a differential effect. The example in Ravenglass Museum is one of the oldest bogies in existence.

A 16-seat open coach used the same layout to carry a ton of passengers for a ton of coach. The design was repeated for Duffield and Eaton, while a 20-seat version on improved bogies is currently the Ravenglass standard. From these practical coaches developed the whimsical Dining and Sleeping Cars completed for the 1894 Open Days. Eight people sat at four tables in the diner with service from the kitchen with its Rippingill paraffin stove. It was used to entertain friends, while the sleeper was an overflow bedroom with four berths, washbasins and dressing table. Initially the Eaton Railway ran mixed trains with a standard open, a parcels van and two brakevans, but by 1911, a splendidly upholstered pitchpine saloon was com-

pleted fully 6ft high. The Eaton open, saloon and both brakes still survive, under restoration at present.

The imported American stock was much lighter in construction to give the tiny Cagney engines a reasonable payload. Blakesley began with the earliest four-wheel pattern, quickly altered there so that three coach bodies sat on a simple railbuilt chassis with bogies to run better on curves. Later Cagney vehicles were eight-seat bogie coaches with awnings like the old 'Surrey with a fringe on the top', partly to shelter fair complexions from the sun and partly from cinders. Bassett-Lowke quickly learned that lesson, fitting roofs and end screens to his 12-seat bogie opens at Blackpool to avoid fire damage among passengers! Greenly also learned about stability when injured in a derailment at White City in 1909, caused by workmen hanging out on a bend. Rhyl saw the introduction of the distinctive teak Bassett-Lowke eight-seat four wheeler, with its low centre of gravity influenced by Greenly. They were supplied to Geneva, Staughton Manor and Sand Hutton and all these eventually came to Eskdale.

Although the mountainous route through Eskdale taxed the small engines beyond the limit, this design of rolling stock was ideal, augmented at peak periods by resort to the old 3ft gauge custom of sweeping out wagons and fitting temporary benches! After the acquisition of the Heywood stock, including the diner, (though it was never used as hoped for to serve

(*Opposite above*)
Cloche hats and Bassett-Lowke four-wheeled coaches at Dalegarth circa 1930. The locomotive is RER ICL No 1. (*Courtesy National Railway Museum*)

(*below*)
The original *River Mite* eases its train of seven Heywood type vehicles over the 'Big Points' at Murthwaite. The Duffield Bank sleeping car is the last vehicle in the train in this 1930 picture. (*Mary Fair*)

teas en route), both it and the sleeper were converted as part of a rake of seven saloon coaches for wet weather use. By 1939 only the diner and one other survived as quarrymen's coaches, leaving the line with no wet weather stock at all. Instead there were three rakes of 16-seat opens, locally built from old ship's dunnage.

Greenly drew on the Eskdale experience in designing the more popular open stock for the Romney, Hythe & Dymchurch project. The eight-seat four-wheelers had well frames for maximum stability in strong winds, and roofs because of restricted bridge clearances, but proved draughty for most weather conditions without glazing in the sides. They were ideal for moving vast summer crowds as their low weight enabled trains of 20 to be hauled even on plain bearings, but they were sensitive to Romney track and speed. Gradually they had additional glazing and some were articulated using Gibbins bogies, but they were displaced by the arrival of new stock from 1934. In the 1928 Clayton Pullmans Greenly had designed winter coaches that were arguably the finest ever built for the 15in gauge, with full upholstery, droplight windows, 'real' photographs, electric light and steam heating. There were seats for 12 passengers who rode in luxury, with their luggage carried in compartments over the bogies. Like most RHDR engines drawing on LNER design, these coaches had a semblance of Gresley styling in the body side panels. The underframe with dropped centre section became a Romney standard while the Greenly bogies had a sprung bolster. So substantial was construction that tare weight was 2½ tons, no worry on light two-coach winter trains but less useful in summer. New Gibbins bogies also had roller bearings to compensate, while in the 1934 Pullman Plus coaches the designer tried to reduce weight per passenger further by very lightly constructed bodies on shorter bogie chassis. These eight-seat saloons were spacious, comfortable, but sadly even contemporary observers thought them too lightly built to last.

Elsewhere the indestructible teak opens survived for decades; original Bassett-Lowke coaches lasted at Margate until the end, while the Barnes 1912 bogie 'cars de luxe' have survived at Rhyl until recent years. At Yarmouth, Parkinson's stock followed a scale model approach with four-wheel opens like five-plank wagons and a rake of saloons complete with corridor connections. These later went to the Sutton Park line where three more were built to the same design, even to the observation end matching the former driving trailer of the railcar from Yarmouth. This stock ran on Skefco roller bearings, replacing plain bearing stock from Hardwicke Manor which went on to Fairbourne. Fairbourne by the 1960s had some innovative stock including the mobile canteen that was taken to the Ferry terminus daily to supply tea and ice cream. Later Guest built two bogie saloons and a 48-seat four-car articulated set with direct air-operated disc brakes. With smart aluminium bodies, they contrasted with the ragtag hardboard bodies then running on Romney coaches.

Things were even worse at Ravenglass in 1960. The sales prospectus extolled the 'full uninterrupted vision' obtained from the entirely open stock but ignored the uninterrupted passage of rain that damaged receipts in a wet season! Initially after preservation, it was only possible to roof six 1923 four-wheel opens, and regauge three 18in gauge saloons from New Brighton and built for the Jaywick Sands Railway. These gave only a fraction of the seats needed to keep passengers dry on a busy August day. From a 20-seat steel framed open, was developed a series of 20-seat saloons with roller bearing bogies inside the frames Heywood style, aluminium bodies for low weight and maintenance, and doors on one side only to cut out draughts. From 1967, detailed changes have produced guard's coaches, semi-opens, wheelchair coaches and railcar trailers, but the basic design has proved itself. Most trains run with a mixed rake that depends on weather and service levels, but virtually all passengers can sit under cover on the busiest days now. The open 16-seat teak framed 1928 coaches still remain popular in fine weather, but all contemporary softwood opens have been replaced by 20-seat Heywood style opens using timbers from the Murthwaite plant buildings.

The RH&DR meanwhile suffered high maintenance costs with the frequently rebuilt 1934 saloons seating only 8-12 people per coach. The 1928 Clayton Pullmans were being withdrawn after 45 years' service. Policy since 1972 has been to extend old frames to seat 20 in new hardwood bodies, thus reducing the number of vehicles but not the number of seats. Earlier bodies had varnished exteriors, but since 1976,

Typical modern RER stock is hauled by *Bonnie Dundee* on the locomotive's inaugural run in May 1983. A 1969 wooden open coach completes the rake. (*Nick Stanbra*)

aluminium sheathing has been introduced to reduce maintenance further. In the same style are guard's brake vans, semi-opens, a track gang mess coach, the driving trailer and the bar car. The driving trailer is a guard's vehicle with end window, horn, headlight, brake valve and radio to communicate with the diesel locomotive propelling it at the head of the empty school train set. The bar car is the ultimate 15in gauge coach; at 32ft long, it seats 16 in heated luxury around a central servery from which a steward produces refreshments, hot, cold and alcoholic!

Modern minor lines have simple stock of welded steel sections, often quite restricted in space to reduce costs and overall weight, but adequate for a short journey. However for the Liverpool International Garden Festival, Steamtown set up jigs to produce 18 mahogany-bodied semi-opens, and three enclosed coaches with guard's compartment and wheelchair access into the passenger saloon. So sturdy was construction that the gross weight of a full nine coach train – and all trains were as full as possible – was close to the limits of the most powerful 15in gauge locomotives on the Liverpool track. At new homes these coaches should prove as durable as earlier exhibition coaches built for the 1937 Dusseldorf line and still in use at Steamtown and Bressingham. Whatever the changes in society and leisure 'men who daily grumble about the amenities of a comfortable suburban train will be quite happy when seated on a wooden bench in an open car under a shower of cinders or a pall of carbon monoxide'. That remark is still as true as when printed in the *Locomotive Magazine* of 1942.

CHAPTER THIRTEEN

CARRYING THE FREIGHT
Development of wagons

Heywood chose 15in gauge to carry stable passenger vehicles but he also saw its potential for carrying goods. 'A much smaller annual tonnage than has been hitherto deemed worthy of a railway may be profitably thus conveyed'. He aimed to replace the horse and cart over distances of three to four miles where 'a traffic of 5-10,000 tons annually is hauled between two fixed points by a single employer' at such places as a large mansion, institution, quarry or farm. There were advantages in being able to lay tracks among existing buildings to the exact point for loading or unloading wagons.

Constructing the Duffield Bank line involved clearing mature woodland, earthworks and transport of materials like rails and bridging timbers. Heywood found the most useful wagon was a simple four-wheeled flat truck. With cast bolsters and set apart to limit overhang, long loads like the 30ft trestle bridge baulks could be carried. Later he boasted how easily the steel for the coal store that still stands at Eaton Hall, was moved with far greater ease than the 4ft 8½in. Such loads as 16cwt of coal or 22cwt of sand or bricks could be carried in an open 'top' on the same wagon. Two men could lift the top and tip the wagon to empty it as quickly as a tipping truck, a type he regarded a fraud 'as to capacity'. In an exercise 69 tons of coal were moved from Balderton to Eaton in one day, while normal operation four days a week showed 'the cost of haulage is 3d per ton/mile less than the average cost of carting, including interest on capital as well as working expenses'.

Six tipper trucks were in use moving coal for generating and heating at Blakesley Hall. However the line's moment of glory must have been the movement of an 8ton generating set with a 5ton gas engine – 'a fair test for the road'.

The clearest demonstration that a 15in gauge railway could serve as a common carrier came with the conversion of the Eskdale Railway in 1915. Even in decline the 3ft gauge line had moved over a thousand tons of iron ore, granite

and domestic coal every year. Soon all the needs of the valley and its produce, potatoes, wool and timber, was carried in ex Duffield Bank wagons by La'al Ratty. At the end of the Great War, the Nab Gill mine reopened sending 100 tons of iron ore each week for a short time. The most spectacular load must have Lord Rea's car returning for repairs, balanced on timbers between two Heywood flats. Other large loads included 10ft flywheels and 8ton castings for the Murthwaite Crushing Plant in 1923. Construction alone required 2,000 tons of stone, while this quantity was processed every month in operation. Theakston 2 and 1½ton tub wagons were used with tipping gear at the transhipment points at the crusher and main line loading ramp. To speed loading main line wagons, the Yorkshire Engine Co supplied six 6ton bogie hopper wagons in 1928. These were soon redundant when the standard gauge siding was laid through to Murthwaite, improving the capacity of the line to 56,000 tons a year. During the depression the market for high quality stone declined badly and only half this amount was ever moved. However even this required smart operation to keep stone traffic moving on busy summer days. The gaping scar in the fellside is a reminder of the million tons of granite carried by the R&ER before the quarries closed in 1953.

It was expected that the Romney Marsh site would offer all year traffic in shingle, livestock and fish. Greenly provided a variety of wagon types from four-wheel Heywood-type flats to miniature planked side door fish wagons. Two bogie sheep wagons gave 10 sheep the legroom of a Clayton Pullman. They had been designed as 4ton open wagons for construction by Jubbs of Sheffield probably intended for the extended Sand Hutton Light Railway. In the event they only saw use as luggage trucks and carrying milk to the holiday camps, as the extensive exchange facilities laid at New Romney were barely used. Even after the purchase of the R&ER 6ton bogie hoppers, there was only internal ballast for them

The Minimum Gauge concept at work. Coal for Eaton Hall comes up the line from Balderton in Heywood box-wagons. (*F. Wilde*)

to carry most years, until two were incorporated in the armoured train.

The most significant freight carried by the RH&DR was the PLUTO pipe sections from New Romney to 'Dumbo', the site of the camouflaged pumping stations near the Lade. 300ft lengths of pipe were loaded in a pyramid of 60 weighing some 70 tons on a train of 24 gutted coach frames. 'They made up to all appearance a mechanised centipede' sounding 'the clank, clank, clank of hollow metal on the move'. After the war there was a brief revival of shingle traffic using conventional tippers mounted on old coach frames. Those who had to run at night with these unstable out of gauge loads might have echoed Heywood's thoughts on tipping wagons, before traffic ceased in 1951. Now as in the full size, departmental wagons far outlive passenger stock so that genuine Heywood and Greenly originals survive at New Romney along-side purpose-built vehicles for track and construction work. At Ravenglass, traditional Heywood type flats are still used – indeed when asked to supply ballast wagons to the Liverpool International Garden Festival Railway, the R&ER made two new ones. The R&ER was also consulted recently about a proposal to move stone from a quarry near Chichester, using purpose-built hopper wagons on a 15in gauge line to avoid the environmental damage caused by road traffic.

Eaton Light Railway, Balderton.

			Tons.	Cwts.	Qrs.
No. Railway Truck					
No. L. R. Truck	Date _____ 191_				
Description_____					
Where from _____					
Where to _____					
Gross					
Tare					
Weighed by_____					

CHAPTER FOURTEEN

SETTING UP A MINIATURE RAILWAY

Any statutory railway, regardless of gauge, has responsibilities in law and is subject to statutory regulation when the public is involved. When public passenger operation occurs, or a line crosses a highway as small as a footpath, the Department of Transport Railway Inspectorate has powers of supervision. Clause 41 of the 1933 Road & Rail Traffic Act (23 Geo V) states 'A Railway Company which i) proposes to open any railway . . . for the public conveyance of passengers, or ii) any additional line of railway, deviation, station, junction or level crossing directly connected with (such) a railway . . . shall obtain the permission of the Minister. The Minister may direct any such inspection as he considers necessary . . . to decide whether approval ought to be given'.

The Railway Inspectorate is also the agent for the Health and Safety Executive with regard to all non-statutory railways over 350mm (13¾in) gauge, and thus is responsible for anything appertaining to the safety of the public and the health and safety of staff, be they paid or unpaid. The Inspectorate requires proper records of boiler maintenance to be kept, accidents, failures and certain operating incidents to be reported. As sanctions, they may require things to be done within a certain timescale by 'improvement notices' or cease with immediate effect by 'prohibition notices'. The right to run a train service carries the responsibility to fence and exclude the public from the tracks, provide suitable platforms and other facilities and to conduct operations in a safe manner. Minimum requirements include £1 million public liability insurance, continuous automatic brakes, an adequate and simple rule book and the examination of operating staff by competent persons. Statutory requirements can be modified to meet individual cases as long as a railway can be safely operated with regard to speeds and gradients.

Finally the Inspectorate is the authority which executes the Light Railway Orders that are now used to transfer the existing rights and responsibilities of redundant BR trackbeds to new companies by an enabling Act of 1896.

From 1875 Heywood had laid his line without hindrance on his own land at Duffield but clearly saw the obstacle to the spread of light railways in 'crossing or skirting of highways'. Permission granted by a council could be revoked at a stroke so he tried to get a clause in the 1896 Light Railways Act to guarantee arbitration, but in vain. The Grosvenor Estate had no guarantee with the Wrexham Road crossing on the Eaton Railway. In addition the locomotive driver was personally responsible for any infringements at this point.

The pleasure park lines were almost universally on land leased from local authorities. Indeed this is a source of documentary evidence for them. Some lines closed when traffic was poor, but most closed when leases were terminated or limited, for example the thriving lines at Sutton Park and Rhyl. Such problems nearly finished the Eskdale line in its early days. Here the original 1873 Company had been delivered by an Act of 1909 into the hands of its major creditor, Edward Dawson. Thus he was able to lease to Narrow Gauge Railways 'site, lands, buildings and everything appertaining to the said railway except the locomotives and rolling stock'. As a JP he understood his responsibilities to fence the line and 'do all acts and deeds necessary to enable the Company to work trains over the lands over which the trains ran and where the lines or permanent way still remains'. This seems to have satisfied Wills, a solicitor. However Dawson failed to pay a debt to the old receiver, which caused a crisis in 1924, resolved only when Sir Aubrey Brocklebank secured the freehold of the railway lands and then took over NGR.

The Sand Hutton Light Railway Order of 1920 followed exactly the procedure for any LRO. Plans and estimates were presented and subjected to a public inquiry at the Royal Station Hotel, York. Sir Robert Walker explained his belief that 15in gauge could move 50–60,000 tons per annum at 30mph. His solicitor commented that apart from crossing highways, they had no need to trouble the commissioners but

Legal wrangles over this road bridge held up construction of the Lappa Valley Railway. Severn-Lamb 0-6-2T *Zebedee* follows the former GWR trackbed in September 1984. (*Peter van Zeller*)

prefered to have the railway established under statutory powers. 'It was not conceived in a moment of inspired enthusiasm but a well thought out scheme'. There was little opposition and the Order was granted to incorporate the company, purchase land, build the line along and across highways and bridge the navigation of the River Derwent. There were easements of the usual requirements to fence, and have gated

crossings. The Light Railway Commissioners commented 'we . . . hope that the line may serve to show that agricultural light railways . . . can be made and worked so economically as to be directly self supporting'.

The Romney, Hythe & Dymchurch Light Railway found itself up against much stiffer opposition in 1925 though most of this had been resolved by the public inquiry. Clauses in the Order sought to appease various parties. 'The Minister may . . . require the Company to erect and maintain gates across the railway on each side of the road at any level crossing of a public highway'. These would be opened and closed by

Another standard gauge trackbed now used by the Minimum Gauge is the West Buchan Railway. Here Dutch-built 0-4-0 *Chough* leaves Banff Harbour in July 1984. (*West Buchan Railway*)

the train crew. 'Before executing any of the works authorised . . . over, under or within 15ft of any sewers, drains or other works of the Lords Bailiff and Jurats of Romney Marsh Level', they were to give notice. There were powers to lease the line to the Southern Railway, but if use of the railway discontinued for six months, the site would be vested in owners of adjoining land. In contrast by the time of the RHDR (Extension) order officials were falling over themselves to support the scheme. The Inspector of Fisheries thought 'the supply of fish to comparatively distant places as Folkestone, Ashford and Canterbury would be greatly increased' while the District Officer of Coastguards saw 'assistance in case of emergency in getting rocket apparatus at Dungeness along the beach'.

The Beeching cuts of the 1960s left a vast number of trackbeds without rails but nothing has emerged on the scale of the RH&DR. From 1973, it was proposed to relay the former Axminster & Lyme Regis Light Railway and 1½ miles of track were laid from a depot at Combpyne. Problems financing the transfer from BR caused its demise in 1976. At this time

another scheme proposed to extend a 15in track from the southern end of the Steamtown site. It would have crossed fields to the shores of Morecambe Bay for three miles ending at Morecambe Golf Course. Opposition on amenity grounds stopped the scheme after a planning application and public meeting. Another line along the trackbed of the Medina Valley from Cowes to Newport on the Isle of Wight actually got a Light Railway Order but lost backing in the protracted negotiations with local planners.

The schemes that have succeeded have modified their grander aims. Five years of negotiation were needed at Lappa Valley to secure land once belonging to the Newquay to Chacewater branch, and to settle with the local authority for it to maintain a large over-bridge on the line. At the other end of the country, planning for the Maud Junction line found at a late stage that county highways intended to remove all railway bridges. A move to Banff Harbour was not without problems. Local residents had put up garages and washing lines on trackbed now owned by the council. Then an owner of a critical section of land withdrew, forcing a deviation of 400yd on a 1 in 70 gradient. The delays and the extra costs had a serious effect on budgets. Compared with this, establishing a line on one's own land is much simpler whether on the scale of the Rhiw Valley, or the Liverpool International Garden Festival.

CHAPTER FIFTEEN

TRACK CONSTRUCTION AND MAINTENANCE

'The permanent way should be made a thoroughly sound job as it will then cost but little for repairs', wrote Heywood. 'Rail laying . . . is of prime importance to a good road, and a matter that, on narrow gauge lines does not receive the attention it deserves'. He alone of the light railway theorists had rolled his sleeves up to work 'with beater, rammer and crowbar'. The words are as valid today when the safety of the travelling public is the main responsibility of the railway operator.

The problems are the same for any railway; two rails must be kept in correct alignment, in *gauge* with good *line, top* and *cant. Gauge* is 15in + ¼in on points and sharp curves (15⅛in at Romney). *Line* is the longitudinal section avoiding dogleg corners and ensuring smooth transition from straight to curved track. *Top* is the vertical alignment, avoiding dipped joints, especially in one rail alone. *Cant* is the super-elevation of the outer rail on curves to relieve the outward thrust of vehicles at speed, whereas straight track is level across both rails.

The track materials have different roles. The rail is a girder that wears on the head but corrodes in the web. The axle load on the wheelset can deliver a ¾ton impact on the point of contact with each rail. So rail joints need support with fishplates, and sleepers close to but not under the break. All rail sections expand the same in warm weather; the joint should allow movement or the track will buckle. Rail creep caused by trains pulling mainly in one direction, must be resisted by fastenings. They vary according to sleeper types, but to keep rails to gauge must cope with side thrust on curves. Sleepers both support the track and restrain it by their mass, helped by the ballast. This gives elastic resilient support to passing trains, and resistance to side movement.

First Heywood tried 14lb rail on 30 × 5 × 2in sleepers without fish plates but this required 'incessant attention'. With fishplates and larger sleepers, maintenance was reduced while axle loads increased. Rails of various weights from 12 to 22lb were tried at various sleeper spacings 'some parts lasting 5 or 6 years without being touched'. To extend this a cast iron sleeper with the same bearing surface as a wooden sleeper was devised, so that depreciation was limited to wear on rails. A detail of importance was 'that joints should be opposite one another . . . A cross jointed line is not only unpleasant to travel on but is also exceedingly difficult to set up true'.

At Eaton, Heywood directly supervised track-laying. Trains brought ballast and lengths of assembled track, the ballast was rammed solid

A contrast in permanent way. To the left, Heywood cast-iron sleepers and 14lb rail as used at Eaton. To the right, modern RER track with 35lb rail, 'Elastic' spikes and Jarrah sleepers. (*Peter van Zeller*)

true to a level and the track joined up before the next load arrived. 'With a staff of 10 men at the railend, a driver and boy with the train, 6 men loading ballast, 3 men straightening and bending rails, and 3 fixing then in sleepers, 60ft were laid in forty minutes'. After a day or two, the gang then set to packing and finishing embankments, crossings and bridges. In one aspect Heywood economised by using ash ballast and so the track suffered under the four-wheeled *Katie* 'as it never suffers under the six and four-wheeled engines'.

Stone ballast was used on the Blakesley Miniature Railway with 12lb Vignoles section rail on pressed steel sleepers giving a fine looking track that was improved only by the easing of points and curves in 1909 to allow the use of *Blacolvesley*. The Blackpool line of 1905 was also laid in the same materials directly onto the sand dunes. Subsequent lines by Miniature Railways of Great Britain used wooden sleepers with dogspikes or coach screws, as 'the steel sleepers do not give sufficient bearing area unless laid very close together' said Greenly. At Rhyl the two types were mixed, ballasted by shingle.

Part of the attraction of the Eskdale Railway conversion was that some of the existing track materials could be reused. The 3ft gauge line had been closed to passengers since November 1908 after 'the Board of Trade had been apprised somehow or other that the line was not what it ought to be in point of repair' according to the Receiver. In fact he had relaid a fair amount of the old wrought iron rail with steel from the Gill Force branch and elsewhere. John Wills took charge of conversion but many of the sleepers and all the fishplates needed renewal on the bottom section. Progress was marked off on Cecil J. Allen's survey of 28 August 1915, as the gang reached the 3 mile post by 1 December 1915 and a further quarter mile by New Year.

Above Irton Road, progress was rapid as more of the 3ft gauge sleepers were kept, and trains were running to Beckfoot in April, a month earlier than expected. However the wrought iron rails with their laminated, split heads damaged the stock, whose narrow, more to scale, wheels found any wide to gauge track. One of the most spectacular derailments of 1917 left *Colossus* running as a 4-4-2-2 with tender mounted on a coach frame. Improvements came after the war when 1½ miles of new 25lb rail and fir sleepers

were laid and the old materials ended as reinforcement for the concrete skeleton of Murthwaite crushing plant. For the next seven years considerable investment went into the track with long lengths relaid with Belgian, French and German rail of 25–30lb yd, new sleepers, and tons of granite ballast. When relaid the old alignments were improved by lifting hollows by up to 5ft and cutting into banks like Mill Wood to ease the gradients. By 1930 the line was recorded on a news film in immaculate condition. The tragedy was that in the Depression there was no labour to clean ditches to ensure that the trackbed drained. Rails in soft spots were soon damaged with dipped joints while weeds grew rife and corrosion set in.

Faced with the completely new line at Romney, Greenly drew on his own experiences latterly at Margate in 1920. Work was started at isolated sites across the Marsh where land became available, but after the Light Railway Order was confirmed in May, the gang of 50 worked full tilt to have a single line ready for the Duke of York's visit in August. This involved completing the two 50ft tunnels of the reinforced concrete road bridge at the Warren in 5½ weeks, and the Duke of York's bridge was erected in six days. The cuttings at the Warren proved a source of ballast and sand for construction. The rest of the line was at surface level with 3in of shingle ballast under the sleepers. These were treated fir 9 × 4½ × 36in at 21in spacing. Rail was 25lb American or similar Belgian probably war surplus, and laid quite randomly with short lengths that staggered most of the joints. Super-elevation was given for 25mph running, the maximum specified by the inspecting officer.

Much has been made of Greenly's rolling stock riding badly at speed, but evidence suggests the fault really lay in the track; had not *Green Goddess* 'gone to sleep' at 35mph on test in Eskdale? Greenly later wrote 'one bright foreman thought he could beat the others in mileage laid per month by neglecting the proper drainage of the formation level. The section was soon the worst on the system in the wet summer that followed the opening of the line. To remedy the matter the road had to be entirely remade on a new and well drained foundation at a cost equal to the original outlay.' There was one report of a temporary suspension of traffic.

Certainly when it came to the Dungeness

extension, the first 2½ miles had 9in of beach ballast under the sleepers while the rest was laid directly onto the beach after the surface was cleared. Sand had been used to bind the ballast and 'a good deal more work will be required to ensure lateral stability and a good level . . . with such unsatisfactory ballasting material', reported Lt Col Mount passing it for 15mph running. However he noted that the alignment and level of the track to Hythe 'had been improved considerably'. It had been a mammoth task – 28 miles of track, 1,180 tons of rail, 60,000 sleepers and nearly half a million spikes.

In regular operation at high speeds, clay was soon pumping up into the foundation while the beach ballast did not consolidate – problems even full size permanent way engineers found the hard way. There was an attempt to reballast with crushed shingle in the 1930s, but Howey's answer to the problem was to refine the suspension on rolling stock. Locomotives had leaf springs fitted to the radial axles, and the driving wheels on the Pacifics. For coaches, the Gibbins bogie was adopted following the lead of the Mauritius and Nigerian Railways. Following use on Greenly's saloons, a passenger on a winter train commented 'the Rolls rolls but the coaches ride steadily'. After the second world war, considerable effort had to be put into restoring the track for passenger service. So much rail had been damaged along the Dungeness section that only a single line could be relaid. The track and equipment of the Eaton Railway had been removed to New Romney in 1947 with the intention of using the Heywood sleepers and rail. In the event it was only used for sidings where it can be seen still.

Another line reconstructed after the war was the Dudley Zoo Railway which was regauged to 15in from 10¼in for 1946. Materials were in short supply including suitable timber. H. T. Guest's firm of building contractors made lintels and curbstones, casting the leftovers of each mix into concrete sleepers. To avoid a potential weakness at the fastenings, sleepers had either holes for these inside or outside the rails. They were laid alternately with tie bars to keep the gauge. A programme was started to relay the line at Fairbourne with similar sleepers.

When the R&ER came into the preserved world, the track had been lost since the war in weeds, with lengths so corroded that sunlight glinted visibly through the web! A policy of complete renewal was started in the hope that one day the whole line would be relaid. Since 1963 most years have seen 600yd of rail go into the main line so that this aim would be realised within 25 years. Rail is now standardised on 35lb mines section in 30ft lengths from the local Workington plant. This heavy section has extra weight in the head and keeps a good top. Sleepers since 1967 have been Australian Jarrah, the same size as the cut down British Railways sleepers under the old rail. This work has been helped by the legacy of good ballast revealed by weedkilling, mixed with the grit waste from the crushing plant which has good binding qualities.

Relaying Ratty is akin to the full size in the problems presented. A daily steam service operates up to November, over the winter holiday, and from the end of March with some intermediate weekends. A morning and evening train runs every weekday further restricting time for engineering possession. However a long established team of staff and volunteers can lay and pack up over 120yd in two days. Preparation is all and before the track is split, materials are on site, and sleepers are pre-drilled to a jig for straight and curved track. Elastic spikes, fishplates and bolts are piled. Rails have been through the mobile railbender to give the required curve. The old ballast will have been dug out by volunteers, and wet spots sealed with a layer of granite dust.

'Upabit!' – attention to detail ensures the highest standards of permanent way on 'La'al Ratty'. Here the track gang lift and pack at Rock Point. (*D. M. E. Ferreira*)

At the time chosen, a train is left on both sides of the break to run the service. A couple from the gang armed with crowbars remove dog-spikes, another removes corroded bolts by sledgehammer, poor rail goes for cattle grids, better rail is kept for sidings or patching, together with good sleepers. New sleepers are spaced 10 to a length, with joints close supported. Rails are slid into position while a grease monkey gauges the joint and fastens the greased plates. Then dogging hammers swing fastening down the new dogspikes.

Next the track needs rough packing with shovels. First the inside or low rail is sighted by the ganger lying at eye level with the rail top. He judges the lift needed on the next joint, and watches the packers ram ballast under the sleeper just at the rail. The middle of the length is packed to suit, and work proceeds – joints and middles. The top will then be good enough for all the remaining sleepers to be packed on that side. The outside rail is then lifted with a level to match or give the correct cant for a corner. Again work proceeds with joints and middles, and is finally packed throughout.

The track is then fit to run over, and will be ballasted to the sleeper tops with a wide shoulder on each side to restrain movement. Finally comes the minor adjustments to line and top,

before thorough packing with Kango electric tamping hammers. This may be required again after a season's running but maintenance for several years after should be limited to fishplate greasing.

Other railways have also relaid considerable lengths – Romney facing the backlog of many years' deferred work, and Longleat completely relaying in new heavy materials. However the most remarkable feat of recent years was the completion of the 2½ miles of track for the Liverpool International Garden Festival line. In view of the heavy traffic expected, detailed specifications were made to ensure that contractors unfamiliar with 15in gauge track would give satisfactory results. On an already prepared hardcore bed, 8cm (3¼in) of ballast was to be compacted by roller. Then a further 17.5cm (7in) formed the trackbed on which cut down BR sleepers and 25lb rerolled rail were laid. The job started in August 1983 with 13 weeks for basic completion. Henry Boot & Son won the contract, and had two gangs of 40 to do the work. It was not helped by the many breaks in the track left at the crossings as construction work took place on the rest of the site. In the event the job was satisfactory and stood up to wear considering the reclaimed nature of the site although the hot weather of 1984 caused a few problems with curves expanding out of alignment. It was a matter of regret that one of the finest 15in gauge railways ever laid should have lasted only 5½ months.

Tortuous curves but immaculate permanent way were features of the Garden Festival Railway at Liverpool. Romney and Ravenglass join forces for the final train, 14 October 1984. (*Brian Dobbs*)

CHAPTER SIXTEEN
SIGNALLING AND OPERATION

Although 15in gauge trains are popularly regarded as toys, as Heywood wrote 'there exists the same liability to accident on a narrow gauge line as on one of full size, and it is only by a similar careful observance of proper regulations that serious mishaps will be avoided'. The operation of two trains at Duffield Bank had potential dangers for the staff of mainly young amateurs. That it ran for over 20 years 'in which thousands of passengers have been carried without a single accident' was a credit to all concerned. Miss Effie Heywood recalled 'when two trains were running at one time, one was a slow train and one an express – the slow train pulled up in Manor Copse Station loop line to let the express pass, and again at Tennis Ground. A very strict timetable was kept to, and the two signalboxes were connected by phone'. She and her sisters manned the signalboxes at these

stations which had 7 and 11 levers working the immediate pointwork interlocked with the 12 signals on the line. In contrast the Eaton Railway had no signals or even regulations for working more than one train. But another family entertainment railway at Blakesley had a full set of Sykes Electric Banner signals 'on a similar system to that in use at the St Enoch Station, Glasgow'. Here however the elder girl, Miss Ivy Bartholomew, actually drove the Cagney wearing the appropriate hat!

The signals at Duffield Bank were modelled on those of the North Midland Railway. Here *Effie*, with a train of original wagons passes the signal controlling movements into the 'southern spectacle'. This photograph appears to predate the construction of the long tunnel. (*Sir Oliver Heywood*)

The automatic warning lights of Dymchurch level crossing protect Ravenglass motive power as *Lady Wakefield* passes *River Mite* on the occasion of their southern sojourn in 1980. (*D. M. E. Ferreira*)

Bassett-Lowke catalogues showed beautifully modelled quarter scale signals for instructional purposes, one of which adorned 112 High Holborn for 75 years. The miniature lines with only one engine, like Southport, had them. Where two trains ran on exhibition lines, signals were installed for real. In 1910 at Brussels with poor visibility on the double track, M. Hervé's treadle system detected when trains were clear of each terminus and pulled off signals allowing another to arrive. Points were sprung to allow locomotives to run round and take the left hand road. At Geneva, a signalbox with seven levers controlled a set of points with facing point locks and home and distant signals, to allow two train operation – if two engines ever reached the site.

In complete contrast was the infrequent service of the Eskdale Railway – making main line connections if all went well! The first Easter of 1916 brought 'a number far exceeding the maximum that was dealt with at any time by the old company'. Trains were sent by time interval; the fastest, *Sans Pareil*, first with a light train followed by *Colossus* with the heavy main train. *Katie* brought up the rear, certain not to catch up! The growth of granite traffic and the possible use of passing sidings at Murthwaite, Irton Road, Eskdale Green and Beckfoot Quarry made a complex working timetable necessary. Even in winter 1924, two locomotives worked stone trains and another the passenger turn. To

cope with the busy summer service, a pilotman supervised the crucial Murthwaite/Eskdale Green section and all trains carried marker discs front and rear. Red meant another train following, white signalled all clear. By the period of the standard gauge line to Murthwaite, a dispatcher at Ravenglass issued written tickets and could reach all stations by telephone.

The lines established by Light Railway Order had a schedule written in specifying the basic signalling required – a home signal in each direction at places where trains cross. A distant signal was also required if the home signal could not be seen for a quarter mile. Signal arms weighted to fly to danger in case of a wire breakage and interlocking to the satisfaction of the Minister were also required. When it came to the construction of the RH&DR, Howey went much further in following the Zborowski main line dream. Initially there were signalboxes at Hythe, Palmarsh, Burmarsh, Dymchurch, Holiday Camp, and New Romney. Block working was by telephone omnibus circuit, to Romney signalbox where a set of manual indicators for each block section recorded train entering, and train out of section. New Romney and Hythe had 17 lever frames working points, starting home and distant signals. The interlocking was tested at the inspection when Lt Col Mount picked up the lack of trap points, and insisted on no night running until all signals were lit. Eventually electric lighting was fitted.

On the Dungeness extension, there were blockposts at Greatstone, The Pilot as well as the terminus, all signalled satisfactorily apart from the fish siding. Once Greenly and the Inspector had gone, this elaboration fell into disuse except where signals controlled movements. After the second world war, the telephone block system was kept with train registers although since 1983, a VHF radio link has replaced the actual phone. The now single Dungeness line is worked on the staff and ticket system. Signals were replaced with colour lights from the late 1950s, though two semaphores were returned to Hythe by the present company for sentimental reasons. Another development taken of necessity has been the fitting of flashing red warning lights to road users at road crossings to full Ministry standards after the tragic death of driver Peter Hobson in a collision in 1973.

Fairground and other non statutory railways were not bound by legislation, but frequently operated two train services with only common sense ensuring one train was on the circuit while the other was loading. At Fairbourne and Southport latterly, trains on the single line carried tokens. Points were usually worked by hand levers, and signals were decorative but often useless. A notable exception was the Yarmouth Miniature Railway where the enthusiastic Commander Parkinson built a signalbox overlooking the station, from which points and signals were worked by a hydraulic pump system. There was interlocking and train detection so that signals could not be pulled off when a train was on a protected section. More recently, the one-time North Eastern Railway at Haswell had a delightful NER style box at Central station and a set of preserved signals that included a slotted post semaphore. Other lines used redundant BR signal frames in the boxes built at Ravenglass and Longleat, where the comprehensive signalling eases operations at busy times. Within 20min at Ravenglass, two trains could arrive and two depart, with locomotives being changed or run round, all without much fuss!

There has been a minor revolution in British railway operation that began at Ravenglass signalbox in autumn 1976. The previous year had seen the introduction of staff and ticket working but this was too unwieldy to work the four sections created by the new passing loops. Electric token apparatus would have been costly to install and staff; instead permission was given by the Railway Inspectorate to use VHF radio between each train and one central controller. This was common practice on rural railways in Europe and the 760mm gauge Zillertalbahn regulations were translated to be the basis of the R&ER rule book. Train crews are given a train order for each trip, showing the schedule, crossings with other trains and any warnings. They call control by radio on the locomotive or the back up telephone at stations to get authority to move section by section. Trains are identified by number: *RandER 1* is the first down train in the timetable, even numbers are up trains, extras start at 40 and works trains at 90.

The controller at Ravenglass marks a train graph in red to denote sections a train has been authorised to occupy, and green to show the progress of trains clearing those sections. A record of each day's running thus builds up, while the colours at the bottom of the graph

Former standard gauge signals dwarf *Blacolvesley*, the world's oldest internal combustion engined locomotive, on the North Eastern Railway at Haswell in July 1971. (*Peter van Zeller*)

show the current state of the track. All voice messages to and from Control are tape recorded too. Meanwhile the driver marks his sheet when authority is given to proceed, or any changes are made. The only 'signals' are the reporting boards 200yd outside the loops and the stop boards. Points are weighted to allow automatic crossing of trains. At the maximum four trains can be moving in the sections with trains at each terminus. Changes can be made quickly to cover breakdowns or late connections. This experimental system was demonstrated by the Railway Inspectorate to British Railways Board members in 1980, during the development of Radio Token Block for secondary lines.

Although radio alone had been considered for the Liverpool International Garden Festival Railway, it was clear that an automatic signalling system was needed to control three trains in continuous operation. GEC Ltd installed two-aspect colour-light signals worked by track circuits, the line being divided into six sections, using standard relays as in BR service. An independent set of level crossing warnings were activated by train operated treadles, ringing a bell at the crossing ahead until the barrier had been lowered by the keeper which then gave a white flashing light to the drivers. A solitary semaphore was the home-made setting back signal for the depot, made necessary by the growth of shrubs that obscured the driver's view of a full length train! A full omnibus telephone circuit was installed between every station and signal, but the emergency frequency short wave radio carried by drivers and guards saw more use.

CHAPTER SEVENTEEN

CASE STUDIES

Steam Weekend at Southport

The Lakeside Miniature Railway has operated continuously since 1911. The original line has been extended at both ends to give 1200yd of track. Since 1948 both termini have had twin platforms and run rounds that permit three trains to operate, handling 1000 people an hour to a maximum of 13,000 on one bank holiday. Of the traditional seaside lines it is the busiest and most elaborate, marred for the enthusiast only by the exclusion of steam since 1969. Although the Barlow A4 diesel-electrics have given faithful service for 38 years, it was a happy move to arrange the Steam Weekend of 28/29 March 1983.

One of the attractions of small locomotives is the ease of moving them by road. From Steamtown came Bassett-Lowke Class 10 *George V* and Class 20 *Princess Elizabeth*, joined by Class 30 *Synolda* from Ravenglass. Remarkably *George V* had opened the line in 1911, while the Class 20 had replaced it in 1913 as *Prince of Wales* remaining until 1969. A pall of smoke once again drifted across the still Marine Lake, Southport's answer to the sea, as electric blowers drew three fires. Brasses were shone, oilboxes filled and tenders heaped with Moroccan anthracite during the hours needed to raise steam. After a trip to test clearances, *Synolda* was coupled to its train, one of the three sets of articulated 12-seat opens. Some still carry plates from the Far Tottering and Oystercreek Railway and all use the special ball joint coupling for slick operation. The start past the shed is gentle enough but after collecting the single line token, the driver must open up for the bank. Under the 'very realistic' tunnel the exhaust echoes back and speed can rise to 12mph before the train reaches the pier. A sharp curve leads into the cutting dug for the 1948 extension, under yet another bridge into Happyland. The driver must stop exactly to clear the points for running round. In reverse the line has a different character; a short sharp pull round the check-railed curve to the pier, followed by a long romp downhill, slowing to hand over the token at the points and stopping precisely in front of the Glass Coach Shed.

Lizzie left, tackling the bank with almost familiarity, giving barely enough time to fill *Synolda*'s tender before train and token returned. After this *George* and *Lizzie* ran double-headed, making a fine sight when passing the diesels outside the shed. Sadly the trip found places that would not allow *George*'s fine scale wheels to pass, and a gang was sent to respike the tight corner.

Sunday was a repeat until traffic boomed and it was decided to run a third train with the diesel *Prince Charles*. For this movement a pilotman was sent with the steam train to operate the points at Happyland station throat. After an interval, *Charlie* followed up to the corner from where it was signalled into the station. The pilotman took its staff to the other train which departed, while the diesel awaited the arrival of the next train. The Barlow diesel is straightforward to drive, hence its popularity in the past. On the locomotive is a direction switch and vacuum brake, while the tender has the hand throttle for the Ford D driving the generator. The trick is to open up just until the motor starts to turn, wait to give a smooth start, then increase power to full throttle to climb the bank.

At such events passengers often have history to recall; one had been a student driver for Griffin Llewelyn, another was Harry Barlow himself. He recalled the instruction 'you needed a pound of tallow and a pound of lard every day – tallow for the locomotive lubricators, lard for the little boys who wedged their heads in the turnstiles!' Finally at the end came a grand finale with *Synolda* and *Lizzie* running double headed. As the photographers took their final shots, a chance conversation revealed that the remains of Class 10 *Red Dragon* were living on borrowed time. Shortly after they arrived at Southport for eventual restoration; such are the vagaries of life.

RandER 10

Just after eight, Ravenglass shed echoes as drivers shovel out the ashes of yesterday's fires;

Four generations at Southport. The original steam locomotives pass their diesel successors at the celebratory
weekend in March 1983. (*Peter van Zeller*)

small locomotives steam best with a new fire on a
clean grate and ashpan. *Esk*'s boiler has no
steam but half a glass of near boiling water from
the day before. Flaming rags, an armful of wood
and half a hundredweight of coal follow each
other into the firebox. Steamraising takes a
couple of hours but the time is used fruitfully to
polish brasses. Bull, maybe, but it pleases the
customers. Next to wheels and rods, every spoke
and rod is wiped, every nut and pin tested for
security. Each driver knows the weak points of
his engine and the consequences. Meanwhile
from the simmering sounds pressure builds up
to the 30lb/sq in needed to work the blower to
draw the fire to get full pressure. Finally paint-
work is washed and the dome polished before
leaving the shed. Backing into the station, air
pump and radio can be tested 'River Esk to
Randerbase – timecheck please.'

The volunteer guard couples up to the four
opens and five covereds, and the air brake
system is pumped up to 50lb/sq in for a

continuity test. Now there is time to oil round,
make the fire ready and fill the boiler before
Control orders appear, the road is set and the
guard's whistle sounds. Reverser in full forward,
whistle in response to the right away, the
regulator is gently tapped – no pilot valve here.
As the locomotive pulls past the sheds, the
gradient falls away, so that the train is soon
rolling down to sea level. Ahead is a panorama of
the high fells so clear it must rain soon. Now the
fire is livened up and may need building for the
climb ahead. Some fuels such as the traditional
coke and some anthracite may be burned in such
a deep bed as to go the full length of the line
without attention. Other smokier coals need a
shallow dished bed and a little top air. The gas
producer system of *Esk* admits half the air over
the fire to avoid lifting the fire and to consume
all smoke.

Through Muncaster Mill bridge, an empty
platform means a good run at Mill Wood's 1 in
42 grade curving through the trees. Before *Esk*,
passengers pushed up here, even *Esk* needs
sand sometimes. By the boat shelter at the top
is the report board for Miteside loop, where
drivers contact control. 'RandER 10 may

Date	29-5-86		Driver	Peter	
Controller	NGW		Guard	David	

RANDER   10

Schedule	Xings		Authority	Warnings etc.
11·50		Ravenglass		Glyn walking length
12·00	x 7	Miteside	↓	
12·15	x/ cancelled by radio	Irton Road		4½m Benny about
12·25	x 9	Fisherground		
12·35	x 9 cancelled by radio	Dalegarth		

R&ER train control order (sample).

proceed to Irton Road'. Over the loop points at 5mph, the train passes a down train behind sister locomotive *River Mite*, and the driver reports out of the first section as the loop point indicator falls. Now the grade steepens to 1 in 47

at Katie Caddie Corner against the bottom of the Muncaster Fells. It is a long slog up to Murthwaite where the Greenly concrete remains. For half a mile the grade eases before the dramatic bend at Rock Point, 60ft above the River Mite, and the winding climb to Walk Mill summit. Only for a few minutes will the regulator have been at a constant setting or the reverser pulled back, as every easing of the climb is met by feeding water into the boiler with the big injectors. A good glassful is needed here as the locomotive drops down away from the woods towards Irton Road.

The scene at the granite station and overbridge is scarcely changed after a century, though bigger trains passed then. Another passing loop is used at busy periods from which the tracks fall through a gap in the hills into Eskdale proper. At the Green, the station stands on a 1 in 112 gradient but the grade under the road bridge goes up at 1 in 36 against the train. The steepest grade on the line is open and straight and rarely causes problems, unlike the winding curves under trees towards Fisherground. The loop here is built out on a ledge and up trains can take water while awaiting down trains to clear the top section. *Northern Rock* comes the other way; interesting to think that Greenly suggested the type as far back as 1918. From here a careful start is needed past the water tank fed from an old mine, up to Spout House corner and on to Gilbert's Cutting through the raw pink granite. Beckfoot quarry on the left is choked by trees but to the right is the River Esk itself, an apt namesake. Beckfoot Halt is not a good place to stop at the foot of a 1 in 38 under trees but if traffic demands, it is an excuse for a thrash. At the top of the bank the old line to Boot climbed behind the miners' cottages, but our main line turns into the valley to end at the turntable by the road. Just under seven miles in 35min running time to Eskdale (Dalegarth). The old line crossed to the south side of the valley where Howey would have taken his Ambleside extension. Trippers are

'*River Esk* to Rander Base, timecheck please', radio control in operation, Ravenglass 1982. (*Ravenglass & Eskdale Railway*)

always fascinated by turning the locomotive, filling the tank with water, trimming the fire with – 'real coal'!

The road downhill is harder to learn: go too fast over the summits and 20 tons of train soon gathers momentum towards points, level crossings or stations at the bottom of every hill. Each train runs differently according to length and load and it is a 'driving by the seat of the pants' job, judging the airbrake application that will hold speed in check, meaning a reduction of 15-25lb. On the steep downhill sections the water in the boiler must be watched to ensure that there is enough over the firebox; a surge might drop the water level at the back end and uncover the firebox crown – a sin of first magnitude. Firing might be needed to keep the fire in trim, and to build it up running up into Ravenglass if a quick turnround is needed. On the last run the fire can be run down. The stock needs to be shunted away and the engine turned for the last time. On shed the day is not finished as 4cwt of coal is needed for the next day, the ashpan has to be emptied, the smokebox cleared and lubricators filled. The locomotive is parked under the lighting up chimneys, the boiler is filled up, blower shut off, and water gauges blown down. A wet day brings the chore of wiping steel work – and unpaid overtime necessary to keep up appearances. Then the driver washes off the dirt of 12 hours on duty, stretching jarred muscles and replenishing the thirst of a warm job.

Engineman – RH&DR.

The firelighter has steamed the locomotive to 50lb/sq in; now the driver has an hour to make ready, oil round and complete the cleaning left from the night before. Like Ratty, the Romney has one man principally for each locomotive. For 31 years George Barlow ran *Green Goddess*. Out of respect for 'the second most famous engine in the country' after *Flying Scotsman*, a footplate pass ought to be with them, New Romney to Hythe circa 1976. Out of the shed and turned, *Goddess* goes onto the eight new varnished coaches forming the 9:25. The signalman couples up, then the hoarse roar of the big jet lifts the vacuum gauge to 21in. The road is set, colour-lights shine green, and the station master gives the right away. Ahead is turn No 1 – 73 miles with three trips to Hythe and two to Dungeness. With reverser wound fully forward, a flick of the regulator is enough to fill the steam pipes and roll the train into the cloud of steam from the draincocks. The signalman waves to show that all couplings are on the short link and the tailboard is in place.

Goddess and her superheated sisters have a crisper exhaust note to *Esk*. As the train gathers speed, the reverser is wound back to 35% cut-off and the regulator cracked into main valve to give 100lb/sq in in the steam chests. Speed exceeds 20mph as the tracks dip and burrow under the Warren bridge, almost a tunnel barely clearing the cab roof. The fire dances with 'vim and vigour' to the first shovels of coal in the back corners, down each side and up front, leaving the centre hollow for high superheat. The firedoor is closed between each shovelful, which has to be exactly placed, not easy across a dancing footplate. As steam pressure rises, the small feed goes on to keep the water high in the glass and the needle close to the red line. The girders of Collins Bridge roar underneath, then it is time to whistle long and loud for Jefferson Lane crossing. Rolling across into St Mary's Bay platform, the brake is dropped to 15in of vacuum to set the brakes on the train, dropped another few inches then released so that the train stops on a rising vacuum, the brakes just releasing as it does so. Away again, the regulator is handled gently as *Goddess* gets to grips with the bank past Golden Sands.

It is only a mile to Dymchurch where St Mary's road must be treated to a whistle voluntary. The station is still much as Greenly left it, complete with gents' facilities in the footbridge piers. The stationmaster gives the right away for *Goddess* to pull across dyke and road crossing onto a marked grade. Even Greenly found 'with my own *Hercules*, tractive effort . . . is higher than the weight on the wheels justified – careless drivers slipped badly'. Once the train is moving the reverser comes back to 35%. It is straight track to Hoorne's Sewer and Burmarsh road crossing for another whistle and speed reduction. Ahead is the Willop, the racing stretch where superheated steam and 25% cut off give an effortless 25mph. However a head wind can mean steady firing around the box, and steam blowing across the cab spectacles. The locomotive slows again at the New Cut for Botolph's Bridge crossing. The piers of the derelict sheepbridge is George's marker to stop firing so that the fire will be burnt through for standing at Hythe. Ahead a train approaches on the opposite line with a closing speed of 50mph.

The Downs close in on the left, with Palmarsh Gravel Pits on the right, and the Martello Towers guarding the coast beyond. On the outskirts of Hythe is Bob Hobb's hut. Bob drove *Hurricane* for many years, keeping tyres burnished and a multi-pointed star on the smokebox door, but has retired to build 5in gauge locomotives in the hut. The dive under Prince of Wales bridge is sudden, with more buildings close on the south side and the Royal Military Canal on the north. The whistle sounds for footcrossings, greeting Hythe outer home, cleared for Platform 2. Now the regulator is eased to keep the train rolling with the engine's motion cushioned. Under Hythe station roof, the vacuum brake handle is set then dropped to stop by the points. A dash of steam in reverse eases couplings for the signalman to uncouple, then into forward to take *Goddess* over the spring points into the neck. Back up the centre release road beyond the signalbox, to drop back to the turntable. The signalman pushes the locomotive round while George feels crankpins and axle ends for any trace of heating. At last satisfied he draws forward to take water by the box and to clear the ashpan: only 65 miles to go!

Farewell, Liverpool

When the locomotives were delivered it did not seem possible that the Garden Festival could ever be ready. Two years before it had been The Cast Iron Shore, an evil smelling rubbish dump next to an oil storage depot. Three million tons of material had been bulldozed into mountains and valleys, and two and a half miles of 15in gauge railway looped round reverse curves and 1 in 70 gradients to fit. It was like the worst bits of Ratty put together in an attempt to outdo Duffield Bank. Only at the end of site construction could test running begin when the gaps at the level crossings were closed. With rusty rails and stiff coaches, even the most powerful 15in gauge locomotive in the world was reduced to a crawl on the banks. Full regulator and forward gear just kept *Black Prince*'s train moving but it was empty! In the shed, *Samson* was jacked up for side clearances to be enlarged on the bogie for the curves.

Days later *River Irt* had been supplied fresh from a major overhaul at Ravenglass to give a third steam engine in place of *The Bug*. As soon

as steam could be raised, trials began. Close to the track was all manner of contractors' junk which *Irt* was only just squeezing past. Down from the depot, the tracks ran double to divide before Fulwood Station. All platforms had ornate brightly stained wooden shelters, here looking out across the lake to the waterfall. The impressive array of colour-light signals was still being set up, so station masters were dispatching trains by telephone as other staff were practising everything from coupling to waving flags. Every station faced a climbing start, here through a rock cutting to the Mill Station. Staff were practising two minute halts at stations that were interminable without passengers, but soon the train ran on to Festival Hall round the shining dome that was to become a symbol of the site. Sculpted seagulls on a footbridge had made no mess! A platform opposite was served by the railcar shuttle to the Herculaneum entrance. High above, steam from *Black Prince* showed *Irt* where the summit lay. Full regulator was needed up the 1 in 70, round a reverse curve so tight that the rear coach was almost opposite the engine. Along the double track past the depot and over the summit, the gauge glasses revealed how tricky the line was to drive, full one minute, empty the next. Rolling down to Dingle station, the view spread out across the Mersey, then the train ran inland past the Blue Peter Dragon into the tunnel.

Six months later came an opportunity to see the line in full operation shortly before the end. Queues still formed in the pens that had seen nearly two million people wait for a ride at the most popular feature on the site. On the train's arrival, all passengers were encouraged to leave the platform before reloading commenced, taking considerably longer than the two minutes envisaged at the start. The reduction of line capacity this caused brought considerable congestion at times when moving 16,000 people a day at peak periods, the only serious problem in the operation. A footplate pass gave access to familiar territory, *River Irt* alongside Driver Rogers sitting Romney-style behind the vacuum brake on the left. From Festival Hall it was full regulator past the crossings where Worzell Gummidge waited. Everything forward and trust in the Lord to give a good start into the bank. Climbing at 12mph, *Irt* passed a train standing at the depot. *Black Prince* was going inside for lunchtime relief by *Shelagh of Eskdale*.

Bringing the story up to date –
(*above*) 15in gauge Super Power! *River Esk, Northern Chief* and *Green Goddess* hauling the 27 coach *Paxman Jubilee* from New Romney on 2 June 1985. (*P. H. Groom*)

(*below*) Fairbourne Rly No 6 Lilian Walter at the passing loop on 6 November 1985. Head of steel for the 12¼in gauge can be seen in the background. (*P. van Zeller*)

Boiler pressure was steady at 160lb/sq in with the feed on and water high in the glass. Past the intermediate block signal over the summit onto a 1 in 50 down grade. The kick from the accelerating train is familiar and a touch of brake steadied the run into Dingle Station. The radio crackles to inform the driver that the locomotive change of the train ahead was completed and that he would have a clear road from the section ahead. The fire had a little attention before the train was restarted. Around a blind corner the grade increased again into the tunnel past real sandstone outcrops that explain the gradients. Over a second summit, on to the double line where *Shelagh of Eskdale* was lustily starting its train from the intermediate block signal, it was all downhill to Fulwood. After this the run round the millstream to Festival Hall was tame operation. Walking away, the last memory of the site was the shrill sound of locomotive whistles and the exhaust beat counterpoint that added an extra dimension to the flowers. Farewell Liverpool.

ACKNOWLEDGEMENTS

The 15in gauge railway is an elusive study leaving scant traces in official records and conflicting reports from contemporary observers. Even the post card with date stamp is not proof against the touching-up of photographs for sale at other railways. This is not to excuse any mistakes, for which the authors accept sole responsibility, simply to explain the special difficulty faced when dealing with these non-statutory railways which most were. Just a handful were constructed under the formal procedures laid down by Parliament.

It must never be forgotten that the 15in gauge railway has given much honest pleasure to ordinary people for over a century – few of man's creations can claim so much. To echo George Barlow of the Romney, Hythe & Dymchurch Railway, it has been an honour and privilege to be involved with 15in gauge railways and sincere thanks for help given are extended to the staffs and managements of the Ravenglass & Eskdale, Romney, Hythe & Dymchurch, Liverpool International Garden Festival and Southport Lakeside, railways. Special thanks are also due to John Harrison, Arnold Staples, Simon Townsend and Dr John Coiley and the staff of the National Railway Museum, particularly John Edgington, Phil Atkins and Chris Hogg. The Model & Allied Press has been very helpful and Ernest Steel and Mrs Elenora Steel kindly gave permission to use material from the Greenly archives. Help with pictures and information has also been given by Andy Anderson, George Barlow, John Batts, A. Booth, R. A. Bowen, Harold Bowtell, Derek Brough, Howard Clayton, David Curwen, W. J. K. Davies, R. Dolling, Raymond Dunn, Douglas Ferreira, Mike Green, H. T. Guest, Emile Gamba, John Hayton, J. T. Holder, David Holroyd, Sir Oliver Heywood, John Henderson, M. Jacot, Tom Jones, Matthew Kerr, Winston Kime, Phil Kingston, Richard Kirkman, Yasuo Koda, G. Limb, Ian McKenzie, Gervase Markham, I. G. Murray, Michael Oliver, Major P. Olver, Jeff Price, Paul Ross, Alex Sangster, John Snell, B. Sheehan, John Stanley, Greville Sockett, Michael Severn-Lamb, John Tidmarsh, Rodney Weaver, H. Wilkinson, J. R. Williams, John H. White Jnr, Jack Woodruffe, Gill Wyatt and E. Youlden of Paxman/GEC.

The book is dedicated to Clare and Kate, without whose patience nothing would have been written.

BIBLIOGRAPHY

Butterell, Robin. *Miniature Railways* (Ian Allan 1966)

Butterell, Robin. *Steam on Britain's Miniature Railways* (Bradford Barton 1976)

Clayton, Howard. *The Duffield Bank and Eaton Railways* (Oakwood Press 1968)

Clayton, Howard; Butterell, Robin; Jacot, Michel. *Miniature Railways* Vol 1, *15 inch gauge* (Oakwood Press 1971)

Davies, W. J. K. *The Ravenglass & Eskdale Railway* (David & Charles 1968 & 1981)

Davies, W. J. K. *The Romney, Hythe & Dymchurch Railway* (David & Charles 1975)

Fuller, Roland. *The Bassett-Lowke Story* (New Cavendish Books 1984)

Hartley, Kenneth. *The Sand Hutton Light Railway* (Narrow Gauge Railway Society 1964 & 1982)

Heywood, Sir Arthur P. *Minimum Gauge Railways* (Private 1881, 1894 & 1898) (Turntable reprint 1976)

Kingston, Philip. *Blakesley Hall and its Miniature Railway* (Private 1981)

Lambert, Anthony J. *Miniature Railways, Past and Present* (David & Charles 1982)

Steel, Elenora and Ernest *The Miniature World of Henry Greenly* (MAP 1973)

Shaw, Frederick. *Little Railways of the World* (Howell-North 1958)

Snell, John. *One Man's Railway* (David and Charles 1983)

Tonks, Eric. *Light and Miniature Railway Locomotives of Great Britain* (Birmingham Loco Soc 1950)

Woodcock, George. *Miniature Steam Locomotives* (David & Charles 1964)

Wilson, B. G. *ABC Miniature Railways* (Ian Allan 1961)

Model Engineer, especially the letters of Henry Greenly
Models, Railways and Locomotives
The Heywood Society *Journal*
Ravenglass & Eskdale Railway Preservation Society *Newsletter*
The Marshlander
The Locomotive, Railway Carriage and Wagon Review.

INDEX

(Page numbers in italics refer to illustrations)